KANPUR 1857

INDIA'S HISTORIC BATTLES:

A SERIES

KANPUR 1857

ANDREW WARD

SERIES EDITED BY

SQN LDR RANA CHHINA (RETD)

HarperCollins *Publishers* India

First published in India by HarperCollins *Publishers* 2022
Building No. 10, Tower A, 4th Floor, DLF Cyber City, Phase II,
Gurugram – 122002
www.harpercollins.co.in

In collaboration with the United Service Institution of India

2 4 6 8 10 9 7 5 3 1

P-ISBN: 978-93-5489-411-4
E-ISBN: 978-93-5489-412-1

Cover design: Saurav Das
Cover illustration: Mohit Suneja

Typeset in 11.5/15.5 Adobe Garamond at
Manipal Technologies Limited, Manipal

Printed and bound at
Nutech Print Services - India

HarperCollinsIn

MIX
Paper
FSC FSC® C010615

This book is produced from independently certified FSC® paper to ensure responsible forest management.

Contents

Series Editor's Note

WARS AND CONQUESTS HAVE FORMED an integral part of India's history since times immemorial. The country is littered with the ruins of empires that dot the geographical map of the subcontinent along with the sites of battles that mark their passing. Yet, the inexorable advance of 'civilization' and accompanying human pressures on the land have led to the gradual obliteration of a large number of these historic landmarks. In my own lifetime, I have seen landscapes change beyond recognition and watched visible markers of periods past get subsumed by unplanned settlements and urban expansion.

This series on India's Historic Battles stems from a desire to better acquaint people with the rich tapestry of India's military history and to generate an awareness of the physical spaces linked to it. The contributing authors have been chosen as much for their passion as their knowledge of the subjects on which they write. While academic rigour has been applied to the research, the tone of the volumes is not academic. On the contrary, it is intended to appeal to the lay reader, while meeting the requirements of the discerning historian as well. In order to do this, each volume follows a common template—an important part of which is the section that provides practical information for visitors who may intend to 'walk the ground' and see for themselves the physical remains of monuments and spaces that were witness to the events described within their pages.

The series will initially cover the sites of the 1857 Uprising in Awadh, Delhi and Meerut, the First Anglo-Sikh war and the epic

Second World War battles of Kohima and Imphal in Northeast India. It is hoped that the series will provide a fillip to 'battlefield tourism' in the country since each volume can function as a stand-alone battlefield guide that will enable the visitor to gain a better understanding of the historical context of important events. It will hopefully also have the effect of generating awareness about the significance of lesser-known historical spaces and monuments, and thereby contribute to their preservation in the long term.

Sqn Ldr Rana Chhina (Retd)
New Delhi, February 2022

Kanpur, 1857

I WAS FIRST EXPOSED TO the events of 1857 as an eleven-year-old boy living in New Delhi during the uprising's centennial. Suddenly, what the British had downplayed as a 'mutiny', Indian nationalists were exalting as the 'First War' of—or for—'Indian Independence', or 'The First Freedom Struggle'. But even though 'mutiny' is too narrow, the latter appellations are too broad.

Though it started out among the Company's soldiers, it was more than a mutiny, but at the same time there are no fundamental parallels between 1857 and the freedom struggle, which, ninety years later, succeeded in achieving independence from Britain by nearly diametrically opposite means, which the nationalists must have implicitly regarded as the Second War for Indian Independence.

The year 1857 was unique in that it was ostensibly led, if not initiated, by the revolutionaries' former rulers fighting for a return to Indian feudalism. Even the word 'Indian' suggests that until the British took charge, India had been one nation that the 1857 uprising was intended to restore. But it was no more one nation than the continent of Europe; and what began in 1857 was almost entirely limited to the Bengal Presidency.

So, I have decided on the rather generic 'Indian Uprising of 1857', which at least gives a nod to its revolutionary aspects but avoids making lofty claims that the historical record cannot support. Arising out of a desire by some sectors to shrug off the East India Company's rule, an uprising it surely was, and under this rubric one can freely integrate not only mutineers, but peasants, landlords, priests, mullahs, rajas and nawabs in every theatre.

But brace yourselves. The Kanpur (then Cawnpore) chapter of the Uprising of 1857 encompasses six of the uprising's pivotal battles, but it tells a tale of such delusion, bigotry, genocidal fanaticism, cruelty, treachery and mayhem that it all but subsumes the acts of mercy, resilience, sacrifice and heroism that punctuate it. The treachery and brutality of the siege of the Cawnpore Entrenchment and its aftermath, followed by the East India Company's rapacious and indiscriminate reprisals, is a story of unremitting horror and devastation in which no Indian nor British apologist should take unalloyed pride.

Grievances

Indian infantry in full dress uniforms. Author's collection.

For almost a century, the Company's Indian troops had served their commanders proudly, faithfully, even worshipfully. But around 1840 a change had come over their officers. John Company had long ago concluded that it could maintain an Indian armed force only so long as it respected its soldiers' religious beliefs.

One of the sepoys' grievances was the rigid and heavy Napoleonic uniforms their officers required of them in the fiery heat. Author's collection.

The generality of the Old Guard had learned their languages, respected their rites and caste and taken pride in their valour and loyalty. But, by the 1850s, the Old Guard was dying out. Back in

Britain, an evangelical revival had enlisted the public in seeking a moral justification for Britain's commercial empire. Many of the young men disembarking in Calcutta (now Kolkata) were convinced by the 'New Lights' of the period that spreading Christianity was their sacred duty: not only to their creed, but to the civilizing mission of the empire itself. Gradually, Indian troops found themselves under the command of a new breed of Company officer who spoke only enough Urdu to bark orders, married British women and derided Indian religion. A few even proselytized among their men.

G.F. Atkinson's 'Our Missionary' expresses the scorn with which the Company establishment regarded the missionaries who ventured into the bazaars to proselytize. Author's collection.

At the same time, British and even American missionary societies had begun to send large numbers of young toilers to India to spread the Gospel. Opening mission stations in Kanpur district; converting orphans and the lowest castes; haranguing Hindus and Moslems

(Muslims) at the city's ghats, temples and mosques—their evangelism was blatant and aggressive, a far cry from the Company's worldly, crapulous chaplains, most of whom could be trusted to have the good taste to keep their religiosity under wraps.

A British couple in the 1870s pose with their baby and servants. From left to right: the khitmutgar, burra sahib, punkah boy, ayah, chota sahib, burra memsahib, and a bearer standing by with a cushion.
Courtesy of Zoë Yalland.

Perhaps just as disruptive was the recent influx of British women. What had come to be called Kampani Jehan or 'John Company' had been almost exclusively a man's world. Reluctant to take responsibility for the safety and welfare of British women, the Company had actively discouraged them from coming to India. But gradually Calcutta bowed to the public's conviction that the presence of British women would have a civilizing effect on their young officers and functionaries, rescuing them from the godless temptations of Indian army life.

The Old Guard's conjugal arrangements had often involved officers installing Indian mistresses or bibis in their bungalows and compounds. This practice had served the Company's interest. In their mistresses' company, officers could cock an ear to rumours from the bazaars; immerse themselves in Indian culture; learn the nuances of the language; and by siring children by them and even marrying them, deepen their roots in India's soil.

'Bibi' in Hindi merely means 'Miss', but among the British it came to mean an Indian mistress. Often housed in separate quarters known as bibighars, they provided the closest thing to domestic life to which an Old Guard bachelor could aspire. They also proved a tough act to follow for the less prepossessing and amenable British women who came to India to find husbands. Courtesy of Wikipedia Commons.

However, as shiploads of British women turned up in Bombay harbour and Calcutta's river port, all that began to change.

Horrified by Indian life, appalled by their countrymen's race-mixing, dissolution and impiety, and affronted that they must compete with Indian women for gentlemen's affections, they denounced bibis as little better than whores. Bibis, in their turn, were appalled by British women showing their faces (not to mention their décolletage) to strangers, even dancing in other men's arms and engaging in affairs.

Hamlah

The courageous and much-decorated Sir Hugh Massy Wheeler posed with his medals and his maimed left arm in a sling. The ominous clouds and the hint of a main guard behind him suggest this is a posthumous portrait. Though he appears to tower, he actually barely broke five feet.
National Army Museum.

At the time of the uprising, some of the Company's Old Guard still held on, among them the commander at Kanpur, General Sir Hugh Massy Wheeler. As Lieutenant Colonel of the 48th Native

Infantry (NI), Wheeler had galloped into the thick of battle, suffering a disabling wound to his left hand from a Sikh tulwar but earning from his adoring men the title Hamlah, or 'attack'. Laying siege to mud forts, subduing brigands and obstreperous rajas, leading the very Sikh army he had helped defeat up into the hills to secure Jammu and Kashmir for John Company, he was cited for his bravery and resourcefulness, decorated, promoted, even knighted.

Sir Hugh had had every reason to expect to cap his career as Commander-in-Chief of the Company's army. But he was perhaps too hands-on and old school: a good man to keep the sepoys in line, but gruff and tongue-tied when called upon to speak; and then, of course, there was the matter of his wife.

Newcomers to Kanpur's military cantonment had to contend with the fact that their general's wife, Lady Francis Marsden Wheeler, was of mixed blood. Initiated sometime in the 1830s, the early period of their romance had been complicated by the fact that she was the estranged wife of a fellow officer. Nevertheless, by the time her husband had been killed in Afghanistan in 1841, she had borne her pint-size suitor several children.[1] Wheeler had been spared the worst of the Afghan expedition, returning to India to help put down an uprising by the Sikh confederacy that had sprung up after the death of Ranjit Singh, the one-eyed leonine king of the Punjab.

Though he complained bitterly to his old friend Henry Lawrence in nearby Lucknow, Wheeler tried to make the best of his posting to Kanpur in June 1856, moving into a splendid bungalow with his wife, two grown daughters and Gordon, his son and aide-de-camp. He inspected his troops, oversaw the construction of new European barracks, and, of an early morning, rode out onto the plains with his children and a pack of hounds to chase down jackals and boar.

The illustrator G.F. Atkinson, who served as a captain during the uprising, depicted himself on his first pig-sticking expedition. Author's collection.

Such was his reputation as a commander of Indian troops that even as the rebellion spread from Meerut to Delhi, Calcutta shared Wheeler's confidence that his men would never turn against their Hamlah. After all, Kanpur was a bulwark against the Marathas, Calcutta's watchtower on the Ganga, John Company's might and main.

A line of Indian cavalry barracks overlooking Kanpur's parade ground. Author's collection.

The City

A colour lithograph from The Illustrated London News. *As a boat laden with wheat passes Kanpur's city ghats, two adjutant storks stand in the shallows, brooding over someone's remains.* Author's collection.

Kanpur had been a town of little import until the British East India Company began to employ it as a staging area for its campaigns against the Maratha confederacy. Over the decades it grew into the Company's second-largest military station, with bungalows, barracks and public buildings rising out of the dust.

Kanpur's famous theatre, photographed before its demolition in 1858. Collection of Mark Probett.

With its races, hunts, balls and theatricals, by 1857 Kanpur had become a comfortable cool-weather outpost for the officer class. The cantonment was centred around a maidan down which, each evening, officers and their families rode their carriages after coolies sprinkled it with water to keep down the dust.

Many of the married officers' compounds featured spectacular flower gardens and fruit trees. Goats trimmed the lawns, and most families kept cows to supply them with milk. Some compounds even contained menageries of monkeys, songbirds and gazelles, and kennels for their imported hounds.

A group of Britons gather on the lawn of a senior civil servant's enormous bungalow in the 1870s, with six domestic servants and two malis (gardeners) looking on. Wikipedia Commons.

Their high-ceilinged bungalows boasted large rooms with polished stone floors and broad verandahs with views of Awadh across the Ganga. Behind the bungalows stood huts that served as servants' quarters. Such households boasted an average of twenty servants, each with a caste-defined task: childcare, cooking, buttling, waiting, driving, toting water, gardening, sweeping, dusting, herding, couriering and so on. Their quarters teemed with wives and children, so that not counting its European occupants, a single compound might have an aggregate Indian population of almost a hundred. During the uprising, such servants would be hunted down not only for defending or hiding their masters, but facilitating the luxuries and conveniences of imperious British families who, had they remained at home on the same income, could have barely afforded to buy a row house in Cheltenham or employ a single housemaid.

The 'Native City'

Behind the jumbled, drab and forbidding facades of Kanpur's 'native city', as the British dubbed it, lived men of considerable wealth: grain and leather merchants, indigo planters, nobles from Awadh, moneylenders so prosperous that in times of trouble the Company itself had turned to them to borrow hundreds of thousands of rupees at high rates of interest to bankroll its campaigns. Then there were the auctioneers who made fortunes putting dead officers' effects and failed estates up for bid: it is estimated that the majority of young Company officers were ruinously indebted to the moneylenders as well.

Almost as prosperous was an upper middle class of hoteliers, printers, dak contractors, brothel keepers and the Eurasians whose import shops catered to the European community.

In a 1927 postcard from Raphael Tuck & Sons, this view of Kanpur's bazaar is intended to depict 'a typical street of an Indian city which has grown into opulence ... Built without plan, it abounds in narrow laneways.' Author's collection.

Otherwise, the bazaars, most dating back fifty years to the city's British occupation, were occupied by a middle class of shopkeepers, tobacconists, barbers, fruit sellers, weavers, tailors and the like, past whose open stalls strolled families from the city and the countryside, as well as peddlers, coolies, waifs, beggars, thieves, and an occasional cadre of off-duty troops. By 1857, Kanpur District's population, both civil and military, had swelled to about 80,000.

Awadh

Lucknow on the Goomtee (Gomti) river, looking towards Kanpur, depicted here as no more than a smudge on the horizon. The destruction of Lucknow in the uprising would cost India its most beautiful and cultivated city.
Author's collection.

In February 1856, Lord Dalhousie, with the wave of a high hand, deposed the king of Awadh. The king's regency had originated with a Shi'a nawab who moved to Lucknow to establish an autonomous domain in 1819, as the Moghul (Mughal) Empire crumbled.

The Company's case against the descendant, Wajid Ali Shah, had been largely trumped up, in the sense that its charges of corruption and incompetence might have been levelled against almost any Indian prince (or European, for that matter). Nevertheless, when the Company broadcast reports of Awadhi landlords (taluqdars) ruinously squeezing their tenants (ryots), the British public was appalled. The king proved incapable or unwilling to satisfy the Company's demands, so Dalhousie exiled Wajid Ali Shah and his family to Calcutta and laid claim to his kingdom.

Whether or not the Company's appropriation may have benefited the ryots, Awadh's powerful taluqdars and Lucknow's Moslem aristocracy were stunned. Accustomed either to defying or making accommodations with the listless king and his agents, now they would have to arrive at a new and less profitable dispensation with a hidebound administration bearing a stranger's face. That the Company appointed the sage and seasoned Henry Lawrence as Awadh's Chief Commissioner was of no comfort to the many sepoys who were themselves ryots. As Company soldiers living under the nawab's rule they had enjoyed an elevated status in their villages and precedence in court, but under the Company's rigid rule, they were to be treated like everyone else.

Rumours

Until the 1850s there had never been much evidence that the British intended, like the later Moghuls, to convert Hindustan to their religion. But with all the changes in John Company's reach and culture, its troops began to subscribe to the rumors that circulated among the bazaars: that the sahibs were circulating flour contaminated with ground pigs' bones and gun cartridges smeared with animal fat, in order to defile Hindus and Moslems, break their caste, and soften them up for conversion.

The year 1857 marked the 100th anniversary of the British victory at Plassey that first established the Company's hegemony. That spring, broadsheets appeared in what the British called the native city, repeating the old Brahminic prophesy that Company rule would last only a single century, after which India would sweep the British into the sea.

In this lithograph by Captain G.F. Atkinson, sepoys dubiously examine and debate the cartridges for their new Enfield Pattern 1853 rifle muskets. The Enfields required that the cartridges be bitten open, and when a rumour circulated (founded in at least one case on fact) that they had been lubricated with pig fat, sepoys darkly suspected that their British officers intended to break their caste. National Army Museum.

When proud sepoys and sowars ventured into town to dine in the roadside dhabas and relax in the chai and sherbet shops, civilians took to taunting them for serving their doomed British masters. Especially wounding were the prostitutes, who refused to service the feringhees' lapdogs.

By May 1857, four Company regiments and a few irregulars were encamped at Kanpur: the 1st, 53rd and 56th Native Infantry (NI), and the 2nd Bengal Cavalry. These were stalwart Company regiments, but there were fissures from the start. To begin with, the regiments were rivalrous, each claiming superior valour to the rest. And within each regiment's ranks, senior non-commissioned officers tended to steadfastly if sentimentally defend their British officers against the accusations of their younger comrades.

The sowars at Kanpur were mostly Moslems who, in the event of a mutiny, intended to ride to Delhi and make common cause with Emperor Bahadur Shah Zafar. Though the Company had rendered the old man emasculate, among Sunnis he remained a papal figure, and to serve him was something approaching a sacred duty.

Emperor Bahadur Shah Zafar of Delhi, the last in a line of all-conquering Turkestani Moghuls that stretched back to Shah Jahan, Akbar, Babar. By 1857, the Company had nibbled away at his power until his suzerainty barely extended beyond the margins of the poems he liked to compose. National Army Museum.

Nana Sahib

No life portraits of Nana Sahib are known to exist. Any such would have been destroyed in the sacking of his palace at Bithur. Or he may have destroyed them himself to prevent his being identified while he was on the run. Several portraits of prominent Kanpur merchants have been mistaken for Nana Sahib's. But this image, which a fastidious Jonah Shepherd—who knew Nana Sahib—included in his Personal Narrative, *jibes with one which remained with Tatya Tope's descendants and comes closest to the verbal descriptions of his guests.* Author's collection.

Kanpur's Hindus, however, had no such figure to unite them. Deposed Maratha princes like Nagpur, Satara, Sambalpur and Jhansi had their adherents. But not until the emergence of the Rani of Jhansi would they inspire much confidence. The deposed Peshwa Baji Rao

II might have fit the bill. Back when the East India Company was merely one of many European concerns vying for the right to trade, the Maratha confederacy he and his predecessors commanded had already disassembled much of the Moghul Empire. But by 1775 the East India Company's machinations had driven a wedge into the Maratha alliance. Forty years and three wars later, the Company had reduced its foes to vassals and banished the Peshwa to the sacred town of Bithur, thirty-nine kilometers from Kanpur, where it could keep an eye on him.

Sly but vacillating, Peshwa Baji Rao II had ultimately, and unwisely, turned against the British and fled when they prevailed. Paying his way through various kingdoms with gifts of solid gold plate, he and his elephants led them a lumbering chase for five months until his capture in 1818. Author's collection.

The mouth of the tunnel on the left in the photo is reputed to have been connected to the Peshwa's palace, down which Baji Rao II would proceed every morning for his ritual bath in the Ganga. If so, this single storey, upon which a residence was built long since, is one of the only structures left standing after the British took the town. Photograph by Andrew Ward.

The terms of Baji Rao's surrender had been generous: the retention of what remained of his treasury, an annual pension of about £80,000 (perhaps seven million in today's pounds), and a six-acre estate.

It was a natural choice. Believed by Hindus to be where Lord Brahma lost a nail from his sandal, Lord Rama was reunited with his consort Sita, their sons were born, and the Ramayana was written, it was far more significant to the people of India than Kanpur, which, for all intents and purposes, had been a British invention.

The largesse to Baji Rao, however, was predicated on an assumption that he was a feeble syphilitic who could not live long. But exile so agreed with His Former Highness that he lived another thirty-three years, enjoying life in an enormous palace that he had built in the austere Maratha style.

In 1827, he adopted a three-year-old boy and named him his heir. Dhondu Pant, known to history as Nana Sahib or Nana Rao, was the child of a family of Brahmins from Konkan on the coast of Maharashtra. By Hindu tradition, adoptive sons had always been recognized as legitimate so that their fathers' funeral pyres could be properly tended. So, when Baji Rao passed away in 1851, his court and religious establishment naturally assumed that the old man's pension would pass to his son.

Governor-General James Andrew Broun-Ramsay, first Marquess of Dalhousie, whose reforms and land grabs outraged India's princes and their subjects. Author's collection.

The relentlessly reforming Governor-General Lord Dalhousie, however, had other ideas. Decreeing that enough was enough, he refused to recognize the twenty-seven-year-old Nana Sahib as the Peshwa's successor, declined to allow him to employ any title whatsoever, and cut off the pension for good.

If allowed to stand, Dalhousie's decree would doom Nana Sahib and his family to subsisting on the Peshwa's dwindling treasury. It would also pauperize the thousands of Hindu pilgrims who had settled in Bithur and depended on Baji Rao's philanthropy to maintain their temples and charities.

Whatever Nana Sahib's personal inclination might have been, his father's widows, courtiers and teeming dependants would not let the matter rest. He was induced to hire lawyers to appeal his case to Calcutta. When that proved to be of no avail, he tried to curry favour with Kanpur's European community, inviting officers and civil servants and their families to his estate for shooting weekends, joining them in his carriage on their evening drives, even joining the local Masonic Lodge.[2] But if any of Kanpur's Europeans put in a good word for their host, it did not advance his case.

Azimullah Khan

It was becoming clear to one of Nana Sahib's most trusted advisors that all this pandering was in vain. Azimullah Khan had a far more intimate knowledge of British pretensions than his liege. An Afghan waif raised in a mission orphanage, he had served as a table servant and tutor for senior officers in Kanpur, spoke impeccable English, and could even play the piano and recite Shakespeare. Exiled from a British household on suspicion of having seduced an officer's daughter, he had slipped off to Bithur and into Nana Sahib's good graces.

A khitmutgar, or table servant, looking much as Azimullah was described. The only known portrait of him was painted in England but was apparently destroyed when Nana Sahib's palace was razed.
Author's collection.

Azimullah proposed that Nana Sahib go over the heads of the Kampani wallas in Calcutta and take his grievance to the British government in London; perhaps even, as befitted Hindu royalty, to Queen Victoria herself. But since Nana Sahib was enjoined by his caste not to cross what Hindus called the 'black water', Azimullah volunteered to sail to London to plead his prince's case.

Arriving in England in 1854 with thousands of his prince's pounds at his disposal, Azimullah's first stop was at the offices of John Stuart Mill, then the Company's liaison officer with the Indian states. Though Mill was not encouraging, nevertheless he found Azimullah so intriguing that he introduced him around to other luminaries, including Dickens, Tennyson and Thackeray, some of whom were openly opposed to British imperialism. At the same time, he would read in the London *Times* editorials warning about the perilous overextension of Britain's armies fighting simultaneous contests in Persia, China, Burma and the Crimea.

Much like this young Indian gentleman, while in England Azimullah donned western clothing, including buckled shoes and a towering top hat. 'Portrait of an Indian Gentleman' by A. Smith, 1841.
Courtesy of Wikipedia Commons.

Azimullah made no headway with the Company or the government. Thoroughly embittered, he seemed fated to return to Bithur a failure. But on his journey back to India, in July 1855 he stopped over in the Crimea to see the British army's condition for himself. What he observed was its military at its all-time worst: bogged down, ill-equipped, disease-ridden and disastrously commanded. So, he returned to Bithur not empty-handed but bearing a new and, to his mind, entirely plausible approach to his prince's dilemma: all-out war against these greedy, calculating island people whose power was all pretence, bluff and cunning.

Nana Sahib apparently was loath to sign on. As a boy, he may have undergone some martial training with sword and bow, but he was no military man. Adept at politics, Konkani Brahmins like himself were enjoined to keep their options open. His brother Bala Rao had apparently acquired a measure of military prowess, but only one of his courtiers, Tatya Tope, would demonstrate a capacity to command.

Azimullah saw that it would take a paroxysm to force Nana Sahib's hand. Whether or not he masterminded what followed or acted merely as an opportunist, by early 1856 Azimullah had ingratiated himself with the Moslem sowars of the 2nd Bengal Cavalry, which had recently encamped at Kanpur. For them, the mutiny in Meerut and its spread to the Moghul capital had a special appeal. When, in May of 1857, their comrades at Meerut and Delhi mutinied and enlisted the emasculate Moghul Emperor in their cause, they wondered what they were doing encamped in dismal, dusty Kanpur when they might join the defenders of their faith in their Emperor's service?

1857 Kanpur Chronology

Note: Italics indicate concurrent events in places other than Kanpur and its vicinity.

10 May *Native troops mutiny at Meerut and advance on Delhi.* General Wheeler agrees to construct a fortification in the cantonment.

13 May *Mutineers at Delhi proclaim Bahadur Shah their emperor.*

17 May Wheeler declares the uprising 'stayed'.

20 May Wheeler's officers sleep in their lines.

21 May Fifty men of the 32nd reach Kanpur.

20 May–3 June *Mutinies at Agra, Mathura, Rohilkhand, Bhurtpore (Bharatpur) and Azamgarh.*

25 May Calcutta promises relief column will reach Kanpur by 19 June.

2 June A Lieutenant Cox is arrested for shooting at a sowar picket.

3 June A British tribunal outrages the sowars by absolving Cox.

4 June *Neill, with one regiment, arrives in Varanasi.*

5 June The sowars of the 2nd Bengal Light Cavalry (BLC) mutiny; joined by sepoys of Kanpur's infantry regiments, they head for Delhi. But Nana Sahib persuades them to return to Kanpur to lay siege.

6 June Entrenchment bombardment begins. *The 6th Bengal Native Infantry (BNI) stationed in Allahabad turns on its officers.*

7–9 June Severe 24-pounder bombardment; Captain Moore assigns a picket of sixteen men to the unfinished barracks.

8 June *In Jhansi, about sixty British men, women and children are massacred.*

9 June The first party of Fatehgarh fugitives reaches Kanpur. Besieged by mutineers and villagers, they are captured.

10 June Heavy casualties: bodies are deposited in a well by the unfinished barracks.

11 June *Neill reaches Allahabad and initiates a reign of terror.*

12 June Sepoys, backed by heavy artillery barrage, are nonetheless driven back from their assault on the Entrenchment with many casualties. The first Fatehgarh party, numbering 128, are brought before Nana Sahib and executed.

13 June Nunne Nawab's gunners inflict heavy casualties by setting fire to the hospital barracks' thatched roof; 100 mutineers are killed by grapeshot as they try to advance in the dark.

14 June *The highly trained Gwalior Contingent mutinies.*

18 June *The 10th BNI mutinies in Fatehgarh, and a second party of fugitives flee by boat down the Ganga.*

18 June *Neill continues his indiscriminate executions in Allahabad.*

19 June Wheeler expects a relief force by this date, as promised by Calcutta. None turn up.

21 June After a cannonball beheads his son and aide-de-camp, Wheeler apparently takes no further part in the defence.

23 June Mutineers suffer heavy losses while mounting a major attack to mark the centennial of the Battle of Plassey.

24 June Nana offers boats and safe passage to Allahabad in return for garrison's surrender.

25 June The garrison agrees to terms. Officers go to the ghat, find the promised boats lack necessities.

26 June Arrangements delay departure. Nana Sahib provides hostages to guarantee ceasefire overnight.

27 June Fatal Day. Garrison departs Entrenchment, walks to boats moored at Sati Chaura Ghat and begins to board, when boatmen set fire to their roofs and sepoys open fire. As sowars range through the shallows, all but 125 women and children are killed.

28–30 June In over two days, the only boat to escape Sati Chaura Ghat floats about thirty kilometres downriver, but gets stuck on a sandbar; the surviving officers surrender. They are brought back to Kanpur and twenty-two men are executed.

29 June Thomson and Delafosse with ten men venture out to disperse sepoys firing from a sand bar but after a skirmish are forced back, and eventually flee to a friendly village. *Neill sends Major Renaud up the Grand Trunk Road from Allahabad with a force of 700.*

30 June *Henry Havelock arrives in Allahabad, finds that Neill has so terrorized the Indian population that he must proceed without adequate transportation. He departs the next day.*

3 July The surviving women and children from the attack at the river are taken from Savada House (or Savada Kothi) and installed in the Bibighar nearby; a second party of Fatehgarh fugitives flee downstream in three boats. On the first day, several are killed: some shot, some drowned.

4 July Thirty-two Fatehgarh fugitives are killed on the river; fourteen are captured and marched back to Fatehgarh. *Sir Henry Lawrence killed in Lucknow.*

9 July Nana Sahib learns Renaud is advancing with only 700 soldiers and sends a third of his army to destroy them.

10 July The remaining survivors from the second Fatehgarh party of fugitives are transported to Kanpur. Four men are spared, the rest executed. The women and children join the captives in the Bibighar.

11 July Teeka Singh and Jwala Pershad lead a force of 3,500 to attack Renaud, but by now Havelock has caught up with him, bringing his combined force to 1,855 and nine guns.

12 July Havelock defeats the rebels outside Fatehpur, fifty-one miles from Kanpur, and commences mass executions in the town.

13 July Nana sends a force under his brother Bala Rao to destroy Havelock's column.

14 July Havelock marches towards Kanpur unopposed.

15 July Slaughter of the captives at the Bibighar claims at least 190 women and children, and four male hostages.

15 July Havelock defeats Bala Rao's forces in the Battle of Aong (Aung).

16 July Havelock defeats 5,000 rebels led by Nana Sahib in the Battle of Aherwa, seven miles from Kanpur.

16 July Bodies of the massacred at the Bibighar are deposited in a well.

17 July An advance party enters Kanpur, finds that all the women and children have been massacred.

18–19 July Hundreds of Havelock's men visit the Bibighar.

20–26 July Havelock's column takes six days crossing the Bridge of Boats into Awadh, leaving Neill in command at Kanpur, where he institutes his 'strange law', executing hundreds by the most debasing means possible.

29 July Havelock takes tremendous losses defeating the rebels in the Battle of Unao, and falls back to the Ganga.

4 August With 257 reinforcements, Havelock again defeats rebels near Unao, but again must fall back.

11 August Havelock makes a last, farewell strike on Unao and returns to Kanpur.

16 August Havelock defeats rebel forces in the Battle of Bithur.

5 September Sir James Outram arrives in Kanpur with a small force, and overrules Neill's 'strange law', but executions continue under civilian 'commissioners'.

19 September Outram and Havelock march on Lucknow.

25 September *The relief force battles its way to the Lucknow Residency but is trapped with the garrison.*

14–15 November Patrick Campbell begins the Second Relief of Lucknow, leaving the command at Kanpur in the hands of Major General Charles Ash Windham.

19 November *After pitched battles through Lucknow's streets, Campbell manages to evacuate the Residency.*

22 November *Campbell withdraws from Lucknow.*

24 November *Havelock dies of dysentery.*

26 November In the Battle of Kanpur, General Windham sends 1,200 men out of the Entrenchment to head off Tatya Tope's advance, but they come under heavy fire and retreat to intermediate positions.

27 November Tatya Tope's artillery opens up on the advance party's two positions, and he takes the city. Windham suffers 315 casualties and orders a wholesale retreat to the Entrenchment.

28 November Colin Campbell reaches the Bridge of Boats, expecting to find safe refuge.

29 November Tatya Tope unleashes his guns on the Entrenchment, tries but fails to destroy the Bridge of Boats before Campbell's men can cross.

6 December After consolidating a force of 5,600, Campbell fools Tatya Tope with a left feint and attacks the contingent on his right, killing hundreds.

7 December After a thirty-hour artillery duel, Tatya Tope sets what's left of the city ablaze and retreats via Bithur.

8 December General Hope Grant advances on Bithur, chases Nana Sahib and his army across the Ganga.

10 December British troops in Bithur begin to raise Nana Sahib's treasures from a palace well; mass executions resume. Kanpur is declared 'pacified', and, except as a staging area for campaigns in other theatres, plays no further significant role in the uprising of 1857.

Fatehgarh

A wary sentry and one of the Nawab's cannon stand guard at the gate to Fatehgarh Fort, a relic of Nawabi and Company rule. It now serves as the Rajput Regimental Centre, and houses the 7th Rajput Battalion that earned honours and suffered tremendous losses defending the British Empire in two world wars. Photograph by P.G.O. Taylor.

No other station, not even Lucknow, was as directly affected by the fall of Kanpur as Fatehgarh, most of whose European community, after an arduous flight down the Ganga, would share the fate of the massacred garrison.

The town itself lay in the shadow of Farrukhabad, whose nawab lived in considerable splendour. Fatehgarh was a drab outpost whose primary mission was to keep an eye on the nawab. But with its entrepreneurial American mission station, indigo plantations, tent and gun-carriage factories, it was emerging as something of an industrial town.

The garrison itself had been commanded by a series of nonentities, the latest being sixty-year-old Lieutenant Colonel George Acklom Smith, whose last battle was thirty-eight years behind him. The only soldiers in his care and keeping were the sepoys of the 10th BNI who were derided by local Indians as the 'Christian Regiment', for having crossed the black water to fight the Burmese.

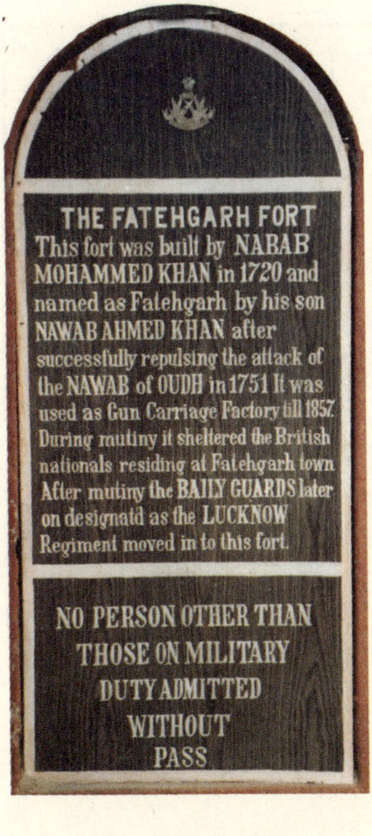

In the spring of 1857, Fatehgarh had become a kind of dumping ground for the most restive Indian soldiers from other stations. However much confidence Wheeler may have placed in his regular troops, the irregular cavalry the Company had organized from the Nawab of Awadh's lancers were another matter. Ill-trained, untested and still smarting from Awadh's

A plaque by the gate to the fort. It did not shelter the British for long. Ultimately 237 of Fatehgarh's Christian men, women and children would die in the uprising, the vast majority in a series of massacres. Photograph by P.J.O. Taylor annexation, they grew so restive that Wheeler sent the most agitated irregulars out of station, ostensibly to aid the Fatehgarh garrison, but actually to defuse their influence among his own men. As they approached Fatehgarh, they proved their disaffection by murdering three of their officers and chasing off a fourth.

Having spent most of his career with the 47th Native Infantry, Smith was an unknown quantity to the sepoys of the 10th and did little to soothe their wounded pride. The majority of his junior officers were bickering, undisciplined, and apparently none too bright. During the crisis that would soon unfold, it is hard to tell whether he failed to keep his subordinates fully informed out of a lack of confidence in them or himself.

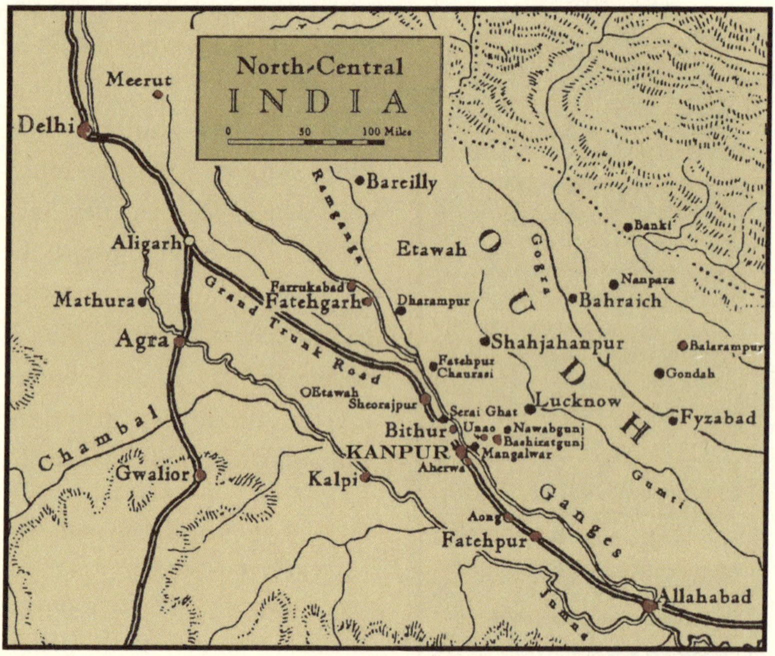

The mutiny theatre from Meerut and Delhi to Allahabad.
Author's collection.

The European community at Fatehgarh was especially terrified by the news of the mutiny in Meerut, and with good reason. Whereas the ratio of European to native troops at Meerut had been one in six, at Fatehgarh there were no European troops at all. It seemed to many in the cantonment that nothing stood in the way of the 10th rising up and exterminating every Christian in the station.

As reports came in that mutineers, armed ryots, marauding herdsmen, banditti and assorted rebels were forming an alliance, Smith instructed the station's European population to listen for his post gun as the signal to flee. But to where? Smith's plan seemed to change from hour to hour: people were to flee to the Colonel's bungalow. Then, no, to the fort. Then not to the fort, to the river.

When guardsmen of the 10th refused to allow the Collector to remove the treasury from the station's vaults, Colonel Smith insisted they were acting not out of disaffection but soldierly pride. Moreover, he declared he was not going to do anything that might further insult his restive sepoys or betray his loss of confidence.

On 31 May, the sepoys stationed at Shahjahanpur, thirty-five miles upriver, rose up, and soon bands of released convicts could be seen skulking along the opposite side of the river. The rebels tried to convince the 10th that like their comrades at Barrackpore and Meerut they were doomed to be disarmed, disgraced, imprisoned, even executed. Smith scolded them for listening to such nonsense and ordered them back to their quarters; and, to assure the 10th of his confidence in them, he slept in the regiment's lines. But his night did not pass peacefully, punctuated as it was by the firing of matchlocks in the bazaars, where villagers and local youths jubilantly prophesized the Company's imminent doom.

Most of the European merchants and their families spent the night on a small fleet of boats that the district magistrate had collected for them along Rani Ghat. It seemed to many of them that their last hope was the river, rising now beneath them through a night of heavy rain.

The largest boat in the fleet was commanded by a relentlessly entrepreneurial merchant named Richard Brierly, who brought along a cargo of wine he hoped to peddle in Kanpur. Other boats dipped and rocked under the weight of twenty-four different families. Scattered among them all were native nursemaids and sweepers and cooks, and in three boats servants and bodyguards sought roosts amid their masters' baggage. By one o'clock in the afternoon some 157 souls had pushed off into the fickle stream of the summer Ganga.

The fugitives' boats were mostly flat-bottomed grain barges with either deck cabins or areas shaded by roofs of planks and thatch. They made good time in the slightly swollen stream, and by the dawn of 4 June had floated twelve miles downriver and landed on the Awadhi bank of the Ganga. The servants had just disembarked to prepare breakfast when four officers of the 10th Infantry appeared upstream, wheeling crazily towards them in a large, unnavigable boat.

Their news was grim. When the 10th Native Infantry learned of the civilians' exodus, hundreds of sepoys swarmed across the parade ground, firing their muskets. During the melee, five officers found themselves cut off from the fort. One of them managed to commandeer a small boat and sail it to the fort, while the other four had jumped into their rudderless barge.

The officers climbed aboard the civilians' boats, and after sitting through the heat of the day they all pushed out into the stream again, peering into the gloaming as the river shredded into rows of narrow channels. Fourteen miles downriver they reached Khudaganj, where rebels lined the cliffs with matchlocks. Their guns flashed with extravagant bursts of gunpowder in the gloom along the cliffs, but the night was so dark that only two men were wounded, including Brierly with a ball to his ribs.

At nine in the morning of 5 June, after Brierly's barge caught up with the rest of the party, the flotilla docked at Meora Ghat, where they met another of Brierly's trading boats making its way upstream from Calcutta with yet another cargo of wine. Hailing his agent aboard, Brierly reluctantly abandoned his wares by the ghat and the fleet pushed on in the midday heat.

The fleet finally divided into two parts: one bound up the Ramganga for refuge in Dharampur, the other continuing down the Ganga for Kanpur under Brierly. The Kanpur-bound party remained docked at Meora Ghat and spent the night of the 5th and most of the 6th reorganizing itself. They decided to shed most of their cargo and consolidate themselves into six of the twelve remaining boats. Brierly led the way with sixty-seven passengers, half of them children, and five smaller vessels bobbed along behind, jammed with women, children, servants, and possessions the party could not—would not—leave behind. But their long halts had given time for word of their approach to precede them.

Seven miles downriver, as their boats bumbled along a shallow, narrow channel between a vast sandbar and the bank of the river, they were met by the inhabitants of the temporary and anarchic settlement of Beloi, who splashed out into the shallows with drums and muskets, surrounding the boats and firing into the air.

Brierly kept his head and ordered the flotilla lashed together by the shore, where villagers kept up their terrifying din until morning. Brierly sent off a servant to learn their intentions. A few hours later, a pair of landlords arrived from an inland village to demand 2,000 rupees.

Seeing there was no help for it, Brierly collected half the sum from his companions and promised the landlords the other half upon their safe arrival in Kanpur. Once his party had cleared Beloi, the day passed uneventfully, but at sunrise on 9 June, as they cautiously floated down to Bithur, muskets opened up on them from the riverbank. Ordering the women and children below deck, several men in the party fired back. But perhaps only three of their shots struck home as they finally drifted out of musket range.

At eight o'clock that night Brierly's overloaded vessel ran aground again, this time on an island from which they could hear artillery thundering in Kanpur's cantonments. Brierly ordered the men to draw the four boats as far into the island's brush and tamarisk grass as they could haul them. While everyone boarded Brierly's boat, he sent a watchman and two servants into the city, the first with a letter for Wheeler, the others to gather information about the rebels' disposition. The servants returned to report that the roads were closed and the garrison under siege.

Through the day and night of 10 June, Brierly's party remained hunkered down on the island, listening to the distant thump and whistle of what they could not know were Nana's guns. The harsh wind resumed during the night and was still blowing on the morning of the 11th as the fugitives nursed their tea. For a day and a night, they had watched antic figures flit obscurely along the shore, pointing, staring, as the fugitives huddled together in Brierly's barge. In the dark they heard noises from across the water—an occasional shout, the stray firing of a musket, the creaking of wheels. Perhaps General Wheeler was on his way, or the rebels were too tied up in the cantonment to bother with a stranded ragtag boatload of civilians.

At about five-thirty in the morning, rebel cannon fired from upriver on the Awadh side of the Ganga, heaving two balls into Brierly's hull. Before the fugitives could jump from the smoking, crumpled barge, a third shot turned the cabin roof to splinters, scattering the party's weapons into the river and crushing to death a Mrs Ives, a child and her ayah. The refugees leaped out and struggled ashore through the tepid, muddy shallows. A few of the men managed to retrieve a shotgun or a rifle as their wives frantically dragged their shrieking children into the grass, seeking whatever declivity they could find.

Brierly's escort now turned coat, setting fire to the boats' thatch and charging around the island, clubbing several of the refugees to death and plundering their corpses. A few shots from the party scattered them, but the rebels only multiplied across the water, cheering as each round of cannon fire raised another spout of sand.

The fugitives could not last long under the broiling sun and ran for the shade of a sparse grove at the southern end of the island, where they stumbled upon a well, but the local landlord would not allow them to use it. Brierly ordered the women and children to return to their hiding places in the grass, and proposed that the men hold a council.

Resistance was obviously useless and escape impossible. So, the few men who had managed to grab weapons now made a show of dashing them against the trees and hurling the pieces into the shallows. But either a boatman's torch or the sheer intensity of the cannonade finally set the grass afire, and in a few moments the strong wind sent it roiling across the island, smothering and burning to death two women and a child.

With a yell, a body of sowars from 2nd Bengal Cavalry raced across the shallows. A local landlord now took charge, and plundered the fugitives of their effects, even their stockings, as the sowars herded the survivors together, bound them with a long rope, and hustled them onto the smallest of their boats, to be transported off the smouldering island and across to the Kanpur side of the Ganga. The inevitable crowd gathered around them as they stumbled up to the road and staggered, shoeless, in the scorching wind to a small manmade pond known as the 'Subadar's Tank', where they remained through the sweltering night.

In the early morning of 12 June, a guard announced that Nana Sahib himself had summoned them to his headquarters at Savada House (also known as Savada Kothi), where their fates would be decided. So, they boarded a train of sixteen bullock carts and rumbled on as a growing, jeering crowd of onlookers crowded around to witness the forbidden, unimaginable spectacle of captive Europeans.

The ruins of Savada House, in which Wheeler had stored munitions. Here the first party of Fatehgarh fugitives were briefly detained, and the survivors of the attack at Sati Chaura, together with both Fatehgarh parties, were imprisoned. An elaborate tent erected just beyond the trees partially visible on the far left served as Nana Sahib's headquarters during the siege.
Courtesy of Tuck Postcards.

As the bullock train neared Savada House, the rebel guns were booming amid the erratic clatter of the garrison's musket fire over a mile to the east. The sepoys herded the refugees inside and seated them on the floor of the large central room, where they remained all morning: relieved to be, at least, out of the sun.

At two o'clock Nana Sahib summoned them out onto the plain between Savada House and the racecourse, and the guards drove the missionaries and the others into a ditch, seating them down in two lines: the men in the back, the women and children in front.

Nana emerged from his tent, a stout man in a tilted turban of golden silk, and walked a few yards past Savada House to inspect his captives. After returning to his tent, he declared to his council that he was disposed to spare his captives. But by this time the mutineers were losing their patience with Nana Sahib. The sowar Teeka Singh told Nana Sahib that unless he wanted the rebels to mutiny against him, he must not deny them a chance to kill these infidels.

In the end, Nana Sahib was probably not so much swayed as worn down by their arguments. Affecting a regal indifference, he apparently washed his hands of the whole business. Through all that followed, he remained in his tent.

As Bala Rao and his fellow courtiers rode out onto the plain, a sepoy dragged the chota sahibs' surviving nursemaids out of the ditch, and held them back some thirty paces from their masters and mistresses. Summoned from the siege line, three hundred armed sowars and sepoys had by now lined up along the rim of the ditch. Once the rest of the crowd had been shooed back, Bala Rao perched himself nearby on a paved platform, and over the missionaries' prayers, the women's pleas, the children's weeping and the merchants' indignant shouts, he gave the order to open fire.

Despite their numbers, it took the mutineers two volleys to still all but a few of the refugees in the ditch, into which the jullads (professional executioners) and a small complement of sowars now skidded down with swords. Some mothers and fathers must have succeeded in shielding their children from the mutineers' fire, for a few children were dragged shrieking from among their parents' corpses and dispatched.

By a little after four o'clock in the afternoon of 12 June, the entire party lay dead. Sweepers moved in to loot the bodies. Some were buried, but most were loaded onto bullock carts and conveyed the next morning to the river, where, until the coming of the rains weeks afterward, their sun-blackened corpses—torn by dogs and vultures, storks and crows—snagged in the shallows and dotted the banks and sandbars.

In early July, after the rebels finally laid siege to what remained of Fatehgarh garrison, a second flotilla of fugitives, including Colonel Smith himself, would blunder downriver, along which the rebels picked off boat after boat until the last remnant, commanded by Colonel Smith himself, was captured near Kanpur by Nana's agents. Three of the seniormost men were spared to serve as bargaining chips, along with a teenaged boy, but their comrades were immediately executed.

The rest of the group joined the women and children who had been incarcerated in a building known as the Bibighar or 'House of the Ladies'. The former residence of a British officer's mistress, it stood about three kilometres north-north eastern of Savada House.

In the meantime, yet another group of captives were executed by order of the Nawab of Farrukhabad. The women and children were fired upon by cannon, the men beheaded on the parade ground, and their bodies dumped in a well.[3]

Wheeler's Entrenchment

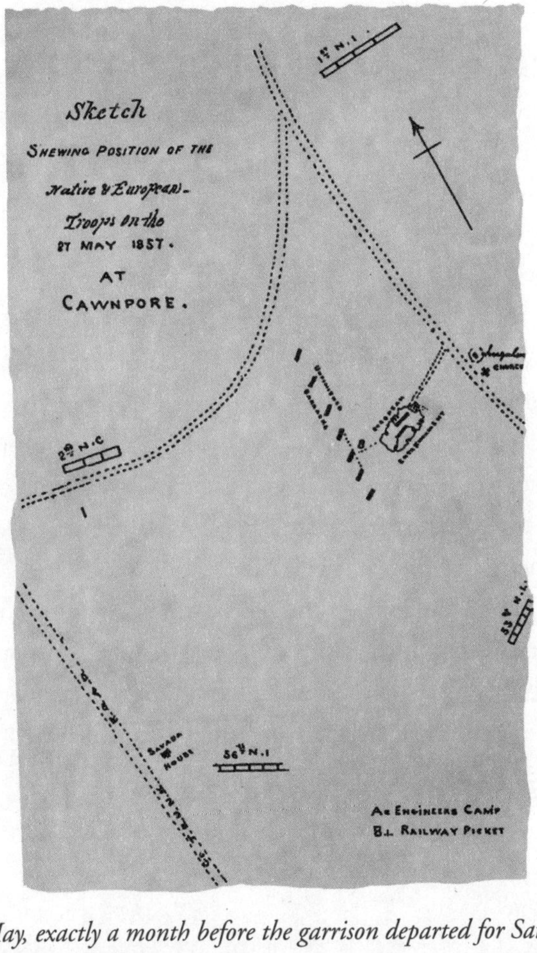

Dated 27 May, exactly a month before the garrison departed for Sati Chaura, this is the earliest known map of Wheeler's Entrenchment. It was drawn by Robert Garrett, a newly arrived young railway engineer who died defending the unfinished barracks. The area marked 'A' is just outside the eastern end of the Entrenchment. Courtesy of the Public Records Office of Northern Ireland.

Wheeler ascribed the outbreaks elsewhere in North India to the panic and incompetence of Company officers who had established no durable bond with their troops. But as bloodied refugees from other stations began to turn up with their tales of massacre and mayhem, the European community became at least as agitated as the Indian regiments. Wheeler received daily reports from clerks and merchants that normally respectful soldiers, peddlers and even servants had begun to taunt them openly and prophesy their doom.

At last, he reluctantly approved the hasty creation of a semi-fortified refuge that came to be called Wheeler's Entrenchment, spread out on the eastern edge of the cantonment. Historians debate why the otherwise sagacious General Wheeler should have chosen to locate the Entrenchment not by the Bridge of Boats, where successive relief forces would later establish their base for the relief of Lucknow, or in the towering armoury nearby, but on a site separated from the city by the restive lines of his Indian regiments.

Some say it was to keep the rebels from observing the garrison's panic. Others that in the event of a siege he wanted to be the first to greet any relief force that might march up from Allahabad. But a few suggest he selected the site half-heartedly because he never imagined his beloved sepoys would turn on him.

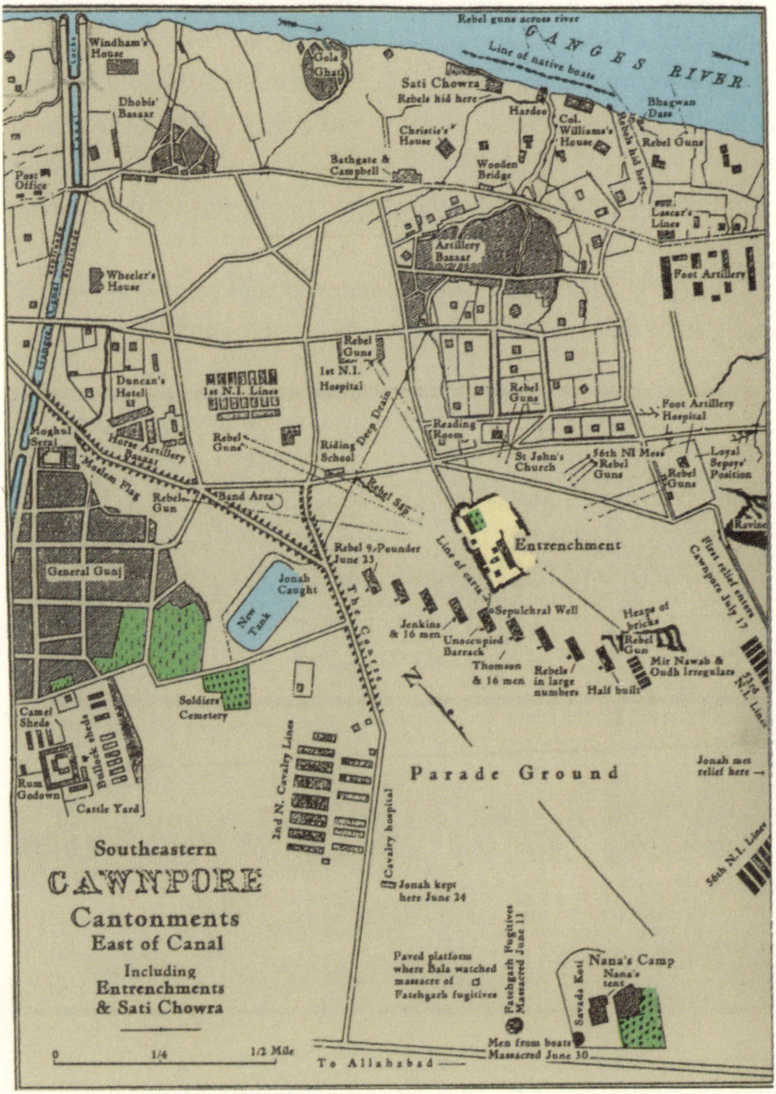

A map of the Cantonments based on W.J. Shepherd's sketch.

Author's collection.

There were other considerations that appeared to have been ignored. For instance, the cantonment was home to most of Kanpur's European families, including, of course, sixty-seven-year-old Wheeler himself. If all hell broke loose, how would they find their way to the armoury or the Bridge of Boats if they had to pass through mutinous regimental camps and the mobs that would inevitably rampage through the native city?

Whatever his reasons—and, under the circumstances, however understandable—it would prove a catastrophic choice.

The Europeans tour Wheeler's Entrenchment. Within a week of mailing off her sketch (top), Emma Halliday, her husband and her daughter would die in the siege. This is the only known first-hand sketch of the Entrenchment before the uprising. In the background are the tents the garrison erected, all of which would soon be cinders. Since the original is difficult to make out in places, I have concocted a tonal version (bottom).
Courtesy of Dr Colin L. Forbes.

Wheeler's Entrenchment encompassed two older barracks, the larger roofed with thatch and serving as a hospital. Drainage ditches emanated from both barracks and fed into a brick drainage tunnel infested with snakes. The Entrenchment boasted only a single well to quench the thirst of a garrison that would exceed 1,000 souls. There was a second well near the unfinished barracks, perhaps one fifty metres from the south-eastern corner of the Entrenchment, but once the siege got under way it did not become accessible until soldiers lined the route with abandoned carts and carriages, and by then it had to serve not as a well but a sepulchre. There were a few other structures: a main guard, huts, kitchens, godowns (storehouses), privies and the like, and some may have been added by the garrison to serve as arsenals and shelters. Otherwise, the Entrenchment was a flat, tamped, sun-struck blank.

These preparations not only disclosed to Wheeler's Indian troops how feeble the sahibs' defences were, but amounted to a betrayal. If the British, as they kept insisting, intended to keep faith with their Indian troops, why would they construct such a fortification? Why would the British order their troops to fetch their wages singly and unarmed if they truly trusted them? And why would they load their guns with shrapnel and aim them at the regimental lines if it wasn't to annihilate them?

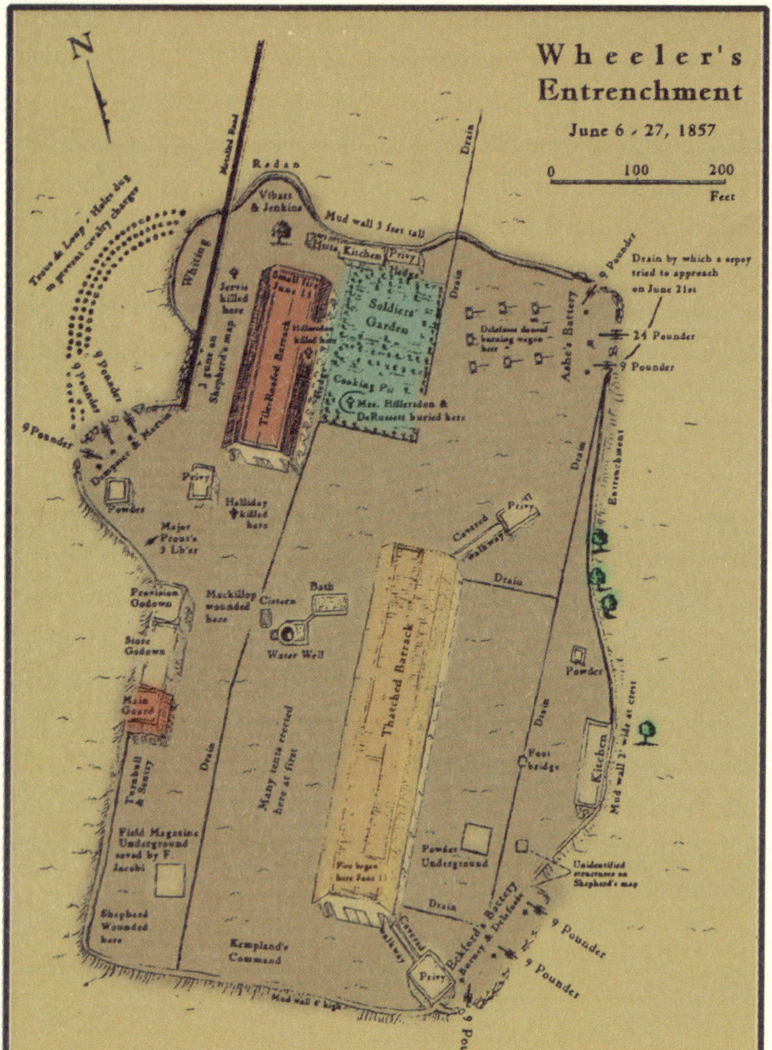

Author's rendering of Wheeler's Entrenchment based on W.J. Shepherd, Mowbray Thomson and other sources. Author's collection.

Alarmed by the news from other stations and the rumours their servants brought them, many Europeans took to spending initially nights and eventually whole days in the Entrenchment. As they sought shelter, the usual hierarchies obtained. The two barracks were reserved for officers and high-ranking civil servants and their families. The rest had to make do on the verandahs or in the ditches along the low walls, where they tried to erect tents and improvise shelters from trunks, blankets, overturned carts and carriages. Except for a few ayahs who cared for the sahibs' children, the servants who stood by their masters had to fend for themselves. European troops and the sepoys who remained with their officers were apparently permitted to find quarters in a portion of the hospital barracks but only until crowded out by the sick and wounded.

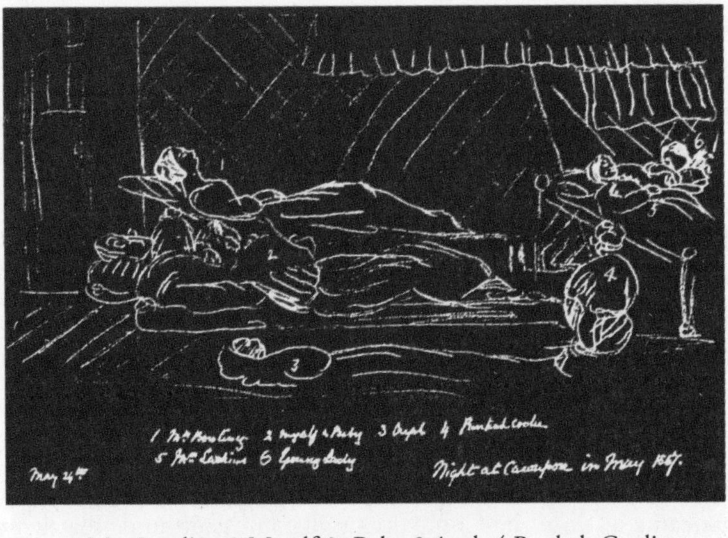

1 Mrs Bowling 2 Myself & Baby 3 Ayah 4 Punkah Coolie
5 Mrs Larkins 6 Young Lady
May 24th Night at Cawnpore in May 1857

Emma Halliday's annotated sketch (inversed) of herself spending the night of 24th May in one of the barracks in Wheeler's Entrenchment. The other memsahibs depicted were Mrs John Price Bowling, wife of an assistant surgeon with the 56th BNI, and Emma Larkins, wife of Colonel of artillery Colonel George Larkins. Courtesy of Colin Forbes.

Jonah

Among the lower classes in the Entrenchment's population were the city's European merchants and Eurasian clerks. The mercantile class, however crucial to the Company's enterprise, were disdained as 'boxwallas' by the Company's officers and senior civil servants who had convinced themselves that they served a higher purpose than the mere turning of profits, whereas the boxwallas had settled in India to enrich themselves. That the same could be said of the Company itself was conveniently disregarded.

Many of the clerks the Company employed were men of mixed British and Indian blood. Some saw themselves as a potentially unifying force, a benign Eurasian ruling class that would eventually reconcile the interests and cultures of Indian and Briton. But being primarily the sons of British fathers and Indian mothers, most were Christians who identified too readily with the feringhee to win over their mothers' people, whereas their fathers' people looked down upon them as feeble mongrels. In short, Briton and Indian each deplored Eurasians for the other's blood.[4]

Among them was a studious soldier's son named William Jonah Shepherd who worked for Kanpur's civilian establishment as a commissariat clerk, keeping the collectorate records of the boatloads of goods that arrived at Kanpur's river port. As such, he was a witness to the sudden reluctance of local merchants to purchase the flour that came in from the Company's mills on the grounds that it was rumoured to contain ground pig bones. No amount of sifting and winnowing could prove the rumour false, and even shopkeepers who were convinced of its purity could find few customers willing to buy it.

Disguised as a tanner named Budloo, William Jonah Shepherd slipped out of the Entrenchment at midday to spy, with Wheeler's blessing, on the enemy's lines. But he immediately aroused the suspicions of the rebels, who clapped him in irons. From his prison cell he would hear the continuing bombardment of the Entrenchment, the clatter of muskets down by the river, and the approach of the relief force. But not until he escaped would he learn that his entire family had been annihilated. Author's collection.

As the storm clouds gathered, Jonah had moved his large family out of the city and quartered them by the parade ground, where he was also a witness to mysterious and sometimes heated arguments among the sepoys. When he tried to determine what they were fighting about, they warned him to keep his distance and protect his family from what was to come.

Shepherd took heed and fled with his family to the Entrenchment, where they managed to find quarters in a room in the main barrack, only to be evicted by a senior officer and forced to seek shelter on the exposed verandah with the rest of the station's outcasts.

The Single Misstep

In this lithograph by Captain G.F. Atkinson, a sowar in civilian dress wielding a tulwar rallies sepoys and golundazes (artillerymen) behind rebel lines. Author's collection.

In one of his last missives, Wheeler at last acknowledged that his situation was so perilous that a single ill-considered misstep on the part of his officers was all it would take to ignite a mutiny.

It was not long in coming. On the night of 2 June, a picket of sowars commanded an inebriated and recently cashiered officer named Cox to identify himself. Still reeling from his revels, Cox drew his pistol instead and fired at them twice, whereupon the sowars seized him and turned him over to his regiment. For an act that would have sent any Indian soldier to the gallows, Cox's brother officers concluded that his pistol had gone off by accident, and dropped all charges. Outraged, Indian soldiers muttered that soon their guns might go off 'by accident' as well.

With Cox's disgraceful exoneration, the precarious balancing act Wheeler had been performing by simultaneously declaring his faith in his troops while preparing for their mutiny had toppled. For the sowars, at least, Cox's exculpation exposed Hamlah's vows of fidelity as hypocrisy and sham.

On 5 June, late in the evening after Cox's release, shots rang out from the camp of the sowars of the 2nd Bengal Cavalry. After cutting down their risaldar (troop commander), they snatched up their regimental colours and prepared their mounts for the flight to Delhi, as their leader, Teeka Singh, galloped among the regimental camps of infantry, enjoining them to mutiny.

Despite—or perhaps because of—their century of service to the Company, the predominantly Moslem sepoys of the 1st BNI needed no convincing and rushed to follow the sowars to Delhi. Apparently, they took the relatively quiescent sepoys of the 56th NI by surprise. Believing the mutiny had already begun, they raced about their lines, not knowing where to turn.

Convinced that their officers had fired upon them, most decided *en masse* to flee Kanpur, whereupon the jittery British mistook their retreat for an attack, and as if to confirm the sepoys' fears, fired at them with their cannon.

'Lieutenant Ashe serving his nine-pounder during the siege'. By firing on and scattering the sepoys of the 53rd BNI who had peaceably if anxiously assembled to see where they stood with their officers. Author's collection.

The crackle of musket-fire raised an alarm among those loyalists who had remained outside the Entrenchment. A mere two weeks before the outbreak at Kanpur, a Lucknow dak contractor named John Hampden Cook had been outraged when his teenaged stepdaughter Amy Horne was teased by local toughs. So he had moved his wife, Amy and her two small stepbrothers and stepsisters to Kanpur's cantonment, where they occupied a bungalow behind St. John's Church. At the sound of gunfire, Cook had roused his sleeping family and hurried them to St. John's, which was itself teeming with scores of British soldiers, Company loyalists and their servants. But now, at the sound of Ashe's initial cannonade, everyone—soldiers, merchants, servants, women, children—tore across 200 yards of exposed ground, flung themselves over the Entrenchment's low wall, and scrambled for refuge along the two barracks' already overcrowded verandahs.

Perhaps the least rebellious of the regiments was the 53rd NI, whose senior officers had kept most of them comparatively calm. But when, as the sun rose, they timorously gathered on the parade ground to demonstrate their fidelity, Lieutenant St. George Ashe of the artillery fired upon them as well.

Nawabgunj

Ever since mid-May, when news reached Kanpur of the uprisings at Meerut and Delhi, Nana Sahib had been playing both sides against the middle. While Azimullah plotted with the native cavalry, Nana Sahib had deployed his own bodyguard to protect the treasury for his frequent house guest, Collector Charles Hillersdon. Had there been no uprising, Nana Sahib might have stood in good stead with the British by maintaining the status quo. But now that the uprising had begun, he greeted the mutineers at the treasury's gates like a host welcoming his house guests. As the soldiers loaded the treasure onto carts, a suspicious Teeka Singh approached Nana Sahib and gave him a stark choice: mount his throne or lose his head.

After receiving Nana Sahib's pledge of good faith, Teeka Singh led the mutineers out of the city. They hoped to reach Delhi in three days, but a few miles on they paused to regroup and confer.

Two sepoys in off-duty dress. One of the first things many mutineers took the opportunity to do was swap their ungainly Company uniforms for more comfortable civilian dress, not only for comfort but to avoid being mistaken for soldiers loyal to the Company. Author's collection.

It was there, in the early hours of 6 June, that Azimullah turned up with Nana Sahib to persuade the mutineers to return to Kanpur to wipe out the garrison cowering in their ludicrous Entrenchment. It would be the work of a mere day or two, after which they could proceed to Delhi in glory and style. He promised to double their pay and, as soon as the garrison fell, to confer on each of their officers a solid gold bangle worth hundreds of rupees. All he asked in return was for them to recognize him as Peshwa and submit to his authority. Teeka Singh and his officers warily agreed to Nana Sahib's bargain, and the mutineers began marching back from whence they had come.

In this illustration from The Illustrated Times, *Wheeler, flanked by Hillersdon, confers with his British and Indian officers as the Entrenchment fills with panicked Europeans.* Courtesy of Zoë Yalland.

With the mutineers' departure, the Europeans crowding in the Entrenchment had taken heart that they might yet live to welcome the British relief force that was said to be marching to their rescue from Allahabad. So, it is hard to imagine their terror when they began to make out the shouts, gunshots and hoofbeats of thousands of rebels returning to Kanpur to lay siege.

The sowars set fire to the civil station and raged through the cantonment, setting the officers' bungalows ablaze until the Entrenchment was flanked by a wall of flame. In the native city they looted shops and hunted down every Christian and anyone suspected of siding with Kampani Jehan. In their clumsy disguises a few Company loyalists who had not yet reached the Entrenchment managed to fool or elude the rebels, but the rest were cut down where they stood.

The Defenders

A definitive count of Wheeler's garrison is difficult to pin down, so it is advisable to precede all of the following figures with an 'about ...' But working from all available sources, it appears that at most there may have been a little over four hundred combatants defending the Entrenchment. The European contingent consisted of fifty-nine gunners, a company of forty-nine men from Her Majesty's 84th, seventy-nine from Her Majesty's 32nd (most of them invalids), fifteen Madras fusiliers, ninety officers of mutinied Indian regiments, twenty-two armed civilians (most from the railway department), forty-three Eurasian musicians. His most effective combatants were apparently his officers and gunners, with the rest taking supporting roles. To what extent the forty-three Eurasian musicians participated is difficult to determine because the Company made it a policy not to train Eurasians in combat. Therefore, they may not have been given arms, at least during the first days of the siege. The number of sepoys who remained in the Entrenchment is sometimes given as 150, but very few turn up on any of the list of casualties. So, bringing the number of sepoys down to a more likely fifty, estimating the number of able-bodied men of the 32nd to have been forty, and more or less discounting the forty-three musicians, Wheeler's effective force at the outbreak of the siege may have been closer to 325, and even that may be exaggerated: Wheeler himself estimated it to be 220. In any case, by the end of the first week, his force had been gravely reduced; especially his exposed gunners, who died in great numbers from sniper fire.

Considering the odds against them, it is extraordinary that they held out as long as they did. The sepoy snipers picked off scores of the men, women and children who ventured out of their shelters, which themselves were battered by the rebels' cannon fire. Wheeler's son Godfrey was decapitated by a rebel cannonball, other officers were disembowelled or crushed under falling bricks.

Charging about, issuing orders, Wheeler's Brigadier died of heat stroke; even deep in the teeming barracks, with few punkahs to cool them down, the heat was excruciating. The only well within reach was constantly exposed to sniper fire, and buckets of water had to be rationed out. The air was filled with dust, gun smoke, swarms of flies, and the dizzying fetor from the inadequate privies combined with the stench of corpses and animal carcasses simmering in the sun. At times there was such constant fire from the rebel batteries that the sound of gunfire combined into one continuous roar.

Scores of the garrison's defenders and their families died of cholera, typhoid, diarrhoea, apoplexy, dysentery and shock. When it proved impossible to bury the dead in the baked earth, a line of carts and crates were strung out between the Entrenchment and a second well to enable burial parties to deposit corpses in its depths. This sepulchre was in turn guarded by squads of officers and railwaymen who occupied two of the nine nearby unfinished barracks, trying to pick off any mutineer who showed his head.

The sepulchral well was memorialized after the uprising by officers of the relief force. The building partially visible to the far left is one of the barracks that Moore and Thomson defended. Courtesy of Mark Probett.

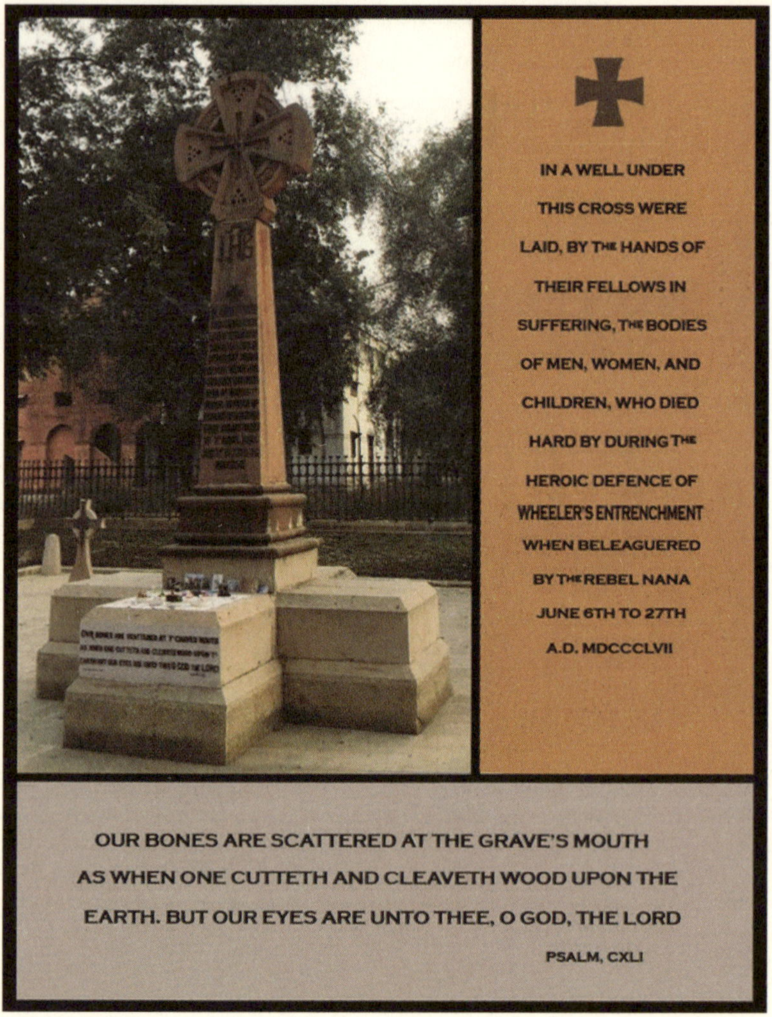

The memorial as it stands today. None of the bodies were disinterred. Visiting the memorial requires special permission of the cantonment authorities. Photograph by Mark Probett.

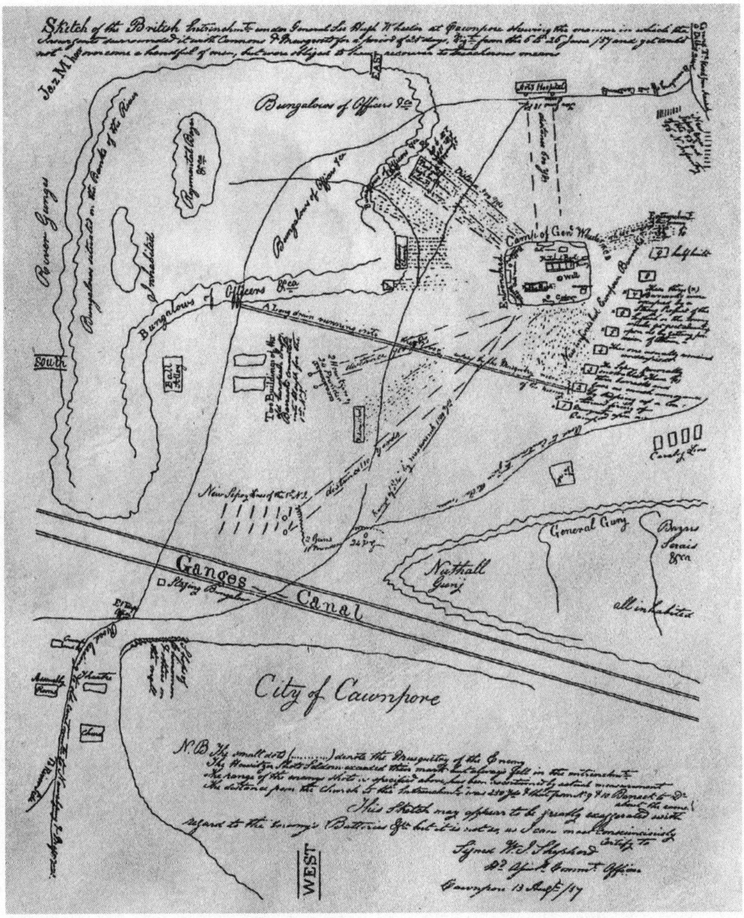

William Jonah Shepherd drew this feverish map of the siege on 13 August 1857 as part of his effort to inform relatives of the fallen about the conditions they endured. It is captioned 'Sketch of the British Entrenchment under General Sir Hugh Wheeler at Cawnpore shewing the manner in which the Insurgents surrounded it with cannon and insurgents for a period of 25 [24] days, from the 5 to 26 [24] June/57 and yet could not overcome a handful of men but were obliged to have recourse to treacherous means … The sketch may appear to be greatly exaggerated with regard to the enemy's Batteries &c., but it is not so, as I can conscienciously [sic] Certify to. Signed, W.J. Shepherd'. Author's collection.

24 June

On 24 June, even as the Lucknow garrison was toasting his health, a sleepless, grieving General Hugh Massy Wheeler scrawled the last of his letters to Henry Lawrence.

'All our carriages more or less disabled,' he reported, 'ammunition short, British spirit alone remains, but it cannot last forever.' Yesterday's cannonade had been 'tremendous', he said. After giving a list of fallen officers and their families, he concluded that he and his garrison had been 'cruelly deserted and left to our fate ... Surely,' he wrote, 'we are not to die like rats in a cage.'

By this time the garrison had lost about a third of its number. Only a little under 700 souls had survived out of the garrison's initial complement of over 1,000; at least 350 men, women and children choked the sepulchral well. Almost every gunner had been killed or wounded, and most of the cannon were too far gone to fire their crews' ingeniously improvised charges of shot. The sentries had barely the strength to lift their muskets and were reduced to using the pages of Bibles for gun-wadding.

But most distressing of all was the condition of the surviving women and children. The burned barrack afforded them only the most precarious shelter, the walls of the pucca barrack were honeycombed; a few more days of bombardment and they would collapse. A rainstorm could dissolve the feeble parapets, foul the muskets, fill the ditches and holes that now provided many of the women and children with their only protection.

As their rations ran out, people desperately improvised meals from whatever came their way. The pickets in the unfinished barracks were reduced to eating dog. 'Our last meal was a Horse,' remembered Amy Horne, plus a small daily allotment of gram. But her starved little brothers and sisters 'would have eaten the most loathesome thing'.

In this twentieth-century imagining of the Entrenchment towards the end of the siege, parched and starving officers and their families huddle in makeshift shelters beside the roofless ruins of the hospital barrack. Author's collection, courtesy of Café Productions.

A White Flag

From the cell they shared at Savada House, the wealthy widows Greenway and Jacobi continued to buy time for their families with promises of ransom. In the afternoon of 24 June, Mrs Greenway was summoned to Nana Sahib's headquarters: a vast complex of curtained rooms erected by the road to Allahabad. In Nana's presence, Azimullah told her that the siege of the Entrenchment had been costly to both sides. He therefore asked if she would convey a letter to General Wheeler.

That evening Nana's batteries ceased firing and for two hours an eerie quiet descended upon the cantonment. Finally, a lookout gazing across the parade ground towards Savada House could see no troops massing in the gloaming, only the solitary figure of an elderly woman waving a 'white wand'.

Ordering his pickets to hold their fire, Lieutenant Mowbray Thomson stepped up to help Mrs Greenway into his barrack. Once she had caught her breath, she handed Thomson a letter addressed 'To the Subjects of Her Most Gracious Majesty Queen Victoria'.

Thomson took it to Captain Moore, who relayed it to Wheeler. Written in English, it said: '*All those who are in no way connected with the acts of Lord Dalhousie, and are willing to lay down their arms, shall receive a safe passage to Allahabad.*'

The General gave the ambiguous little missive a quick, disgusted perusal and thrust it back at Moore, saying he would not dignify any communication that did not bear Nana Sahib's own signature.

So, Mrs Greenway teetered back across the parade ground to tell Nana Sahib he should at least take the trouble to sign his messages.

Moore returned to the barracks to inform Thomson and his pickets that if Nana replied with a signed letter Wheeler might be prepared to treat with him. Wheeler, in the meantime, apprised his officers of the letter, and 'the contents of this craftily worded note'. Thomson wrote disgustedly, 'instead of being kept secret was noised abroad to everyone'. Soon the entire garrison was abuzz.

Many officers declared that they could not trust the gentleman of Bithur, for look what trusting him had already cost them. But most of the women and many of the exhausted sentries disagreed. Thomson watched and listened as Nana Sahib's letter corroded the unity and resolution that had sustained the garrison these three weeks.

By the time Mrs Greenway had returned to Nana Sahib, she was worn out, and the next morning, 25 June, the job of courier fell to Mrs Jacobi. A little after nine, she arrived in the Entrenchment in a dooly (palanquin). Wheeler emerged from the pucca barrack to receive the same letter. Now it bore Nana's full signature, to which

His Highness could not have resisted appending all his restored titles. Wheeler and Moore and the remainder of his senior staff entered the Main Guard together and debated the merits of Nana's overture. Certainly, it could not be accepted without clarifications and guarantees. Offhand it seemed rather hedgy and sly, and it must have occurred to a few alarmists that they had no idea if there could be any such thing as a safe passage to Allahabad. What if the rebels had taken every district along the way? How did they know that Allahabad itself was still in British hands?

Wheeler himself opposed capitulating. He had already been duped once; he was not going to be fooled again. Nor did he intend to end fifty-four years of honourable service by surrendering to a Maratha. He proposed that they all resume their places in the trenches and hold out, as before, until relief finally arrived.

He was not alone. 'Many officers objected to any terms offered by this Nana.' Better to die honourably, they said, than risk his treachery.

But these officers were mostly bachelors and others who had already lost their wives and children in the siege. So, it fell to Captain Moore to argue the case for capitulation. Moore hoped he had demonstrated with his service that he too would sooner die than capitulate. But however much his fellow officers might deplore surrendering, it was the only possible means of preserving the lives of the remaining women and children.

Exhausted by the siege, grieving for his son, fearing for the fate of his wife and two daughters, Wheeler at last 'succumbed to Captain Moore's expostulations, and consented to the preparation of a treaty of capitulation'. If the rebels accepted his terms, he might yet save the women and children, including his own. If not, at least the guns would have been stilled a little while.

Wheeler sent Mrs Jacobi back to Savada House to inform Nana Sahib that the General's senior officers, including Moore, would meet with Nana's representatives in front of the outer barracks. About one o'clock in the afternoon, Azimullah and Brigadier Jwala Pershad accordingly rode out onto the parade ground with a few sowars of the 2nd Bengal Light Cavalry (BLC), and paused 200 yards from Thomson's picket to await Wheeler's delegation. When Moore and his comrades had made their way from the outer barracks, Azimullah greeted them in English to convey his prince's condolences for the frightful sufferings of the women and children.

But his glowering brigadier interrupted him to insist that Azimullah conduct the negotiations in Marathi or not at all. With a helpless, complicitous shrug towards Wheeler's men, Azimullah expanded on Nana's proposal. In exchange for the surrender of the garrison's money, guns and ammunition, Nana would provide the garrison with a flotilla of twenty-four covered boats for their safe passage to Allahabad.

Moore told them that before Wheeler would even consider such a proposition, Nana would have to agree to supply the boats with enough flour to sustain them. Azimullah grandly offered to supply not only flour but 'sheep and goats also'. Moore also insisted on elephants, horses and carts to transport the women, children and wounded the mile to Sati Chaura. In addition, he rejected Nana Sahib's demand that the garrison give up its arms; they would only proceed to the boats with their arms and sixty rounds of ammunition each. Azimullah replied that His Highness would probably agree.

All this must have taken an hour or so, for it was not until mid-afternoon that a sowar returned from Nana Sahib's camp to report that though he agreed to all the conditions negotiated by Azimullah, His Majesty was adding a condition of his own: that the garrison evacuate the Entrenchment that very night. Moore indignantly ordered the sowar to go back to Nana and tell him that the garrison could not possibly leave the Entrenchment until the following day.

The sowar returned to Savada House and after a brief pause came galloping back across the parade ground to warn the garrison that the Nana insisted on an immediate evacuation, and any hesitation would cause his batteries to resume their barrage. Captain Francis Whiting replied that the garrison was not afraid of the rebels. Nana had tried to take the Entrenchment in the past; let him try again. Even if the rebels succeeded, he said, Wheeler had men posted at each of the powder magazines, poised to blow themselves and the rebels to kingdom come if they tried to storm the parapets.

This seemed to confirm the rebels' long standing suspicion that the British had mined the Entrenchment with explosives. The sowar gloomily returned to Savada House, 'and by and by he came out to us again, with the verbal consent that we should delay the embarkation until morning'.

Whiting and Postmaster Roache penned the revised terms of surrender for Moore to sign in Wheeler's stead. A Mr Todd, formerly of the railway department, volunteered to deliver the agreement, having once served as Nana Sahib's tutor. About a half hour later, he returned to report that he had been courteously received and that Nana had signed the treaty without hesitation.

By evening, the rebel guns had been silent for twelve hours, and everyone emerged from their hiding places like resurrected corpses rising from their graves. W. Williamson, Shepherd's superior at the commissariat and now the major of brigade, distributed double rations of chapattis, dal and rum. Their shrunken stomachs swollen with food and water, the garrison lay down for the night for their first unbroken sleep in three weeks.

The Illustrated Times *lithograph of the Entrenchment with labels added identifying the unfinished barracks, the redan, the main guard, and the tile-roofed and thatched barracks.* Author's collection.

The Entrenchment
26 June

In the morning, 'a weight seemed taken off each heart', remembered Amy Horne. 'The joy was general and everybody appeared to have at once forgotten their past sufferings.'

Since Nana intended to provide safe passage that evening, the garrison spent the day preparing for the journey. Most of the women and children had lost everything, but some had retained a few items—Bibles, combs, jewels, cabinet portraits, lockets of hair—which they now tucked under their tattered skirts. All day long sentries crowded the godown to stuff their pockets with cartridges 'till they were walking magazines' and then sat cleaning their muskets and pistols and sharpening their swords and bayonets.

At about two o'clock in the afternoon Nana sent over two elephants and a company of sowars to take a delegation of officers to the river to inspect the boats he had ordered for the garrison's embarkation. Three mutineer officers followed them along the metalled road as they made their way through the encircling crowd of townspeople, servants and mutineers, plodding the mile north-eastward and across a wooden bridge to the dry nullah that led eastward from a low rise known as the Ganga Cliff to the river.

To the right a row of gnarled trees marked the boundary between the dirt road to the water and the deserted riverside compound of the late Colonel Williams. The left bank of the nullah was lined with a row of prickly pear flanked by the walled estate of Henry Christie of Bathgate & Campbell, now four days dead. Below Christie's compound, about a hundred yards upriver from the nullah, lay the boatmen's village of Sati Chaura, sitting low along the bank.

Sati Chaura Ghat as it appeared in 1858, taken from upriver, by the boatmen's village. A ghostly vessel, similar to the boats Nana Sahib provided, sits moored before a line of boatmen's huts. Author's collection.

At the mouth of the nullah, over 300 yards from the road, stood a Shivaite temple patronized by the boatmen of the area. Known as the Hardeo Temple, it was built into the riverbank, its upper level consisting of a domed shrine and two terraces that reached towards the Ganga like the arms of a chair, between which a wide row of steps led down to the water when the river was high.

Captain Athill Turner and his party proceeded on their elephants onto the mud flats to inspect the fleet moored in a long line bisected by the nullah's mouth. There they were met by a boat contractor named Goordial, who accompanied them on their inspection.

Turner protested that only a few of the boats had been supplied with food, and several still lacked proper 'chuppers'—thatched roofs—to protect their passengers from the sun. Goordial bawled out one of Nana's functionaries who had been superintending a crew of 400 coolies from Bithur. His complaint echoed from underling to underling in the usual declension, until the coolies themselves were snapping at each other. But the boatmen must have assumed that whether or not the garrison ever reached Allahabad, they would probably never see their boats again. So they may have contributed only their meanest vessels.

Each required crews of four or five, but only about nine of Nana's vessels had full complements of boatmen, another ten had three; the rest had none. Many were equipped with A-frame thatched roofs that ran almost the entire vessel's length, and though all required oarsmen and pilots to man their tillers, some also boasted masts up which a coarse sail could be raised once they reached deep water. Their hulls floated just clear of the river bottom and were tied to long bamboo poles driven into the mud. The deepest part of the river ran along the Lucknow side of the Ganga, and the officers could see that as soon as the boats were loaded, they must pole their way several hundred yards out into the water before they could catch the current.

Though Turner was evidently reassured to see teams of coolies carting food into the finished boats, he warned Goordial that unless every boat was fitted out satisfactorily the garrison would refuse to board. As the officers' elephants lumbered back up the nullah, sepoys of the 56th walked alongside, conversing with the sowar escort, and unless it was merely a trick of the afternoon wind or the noise from the sparrows flocking in the trees, one officer swore he heard the word 'kuttle' or 'massacre' among the rebels' whispers.

This remarkably comprehensive photograph, taken around the time of the uprising's fiftieth anniversary, provides a retrospection of all that transpired at Sati Chaura Ghat on 27 June 1857. From left to right, as a couple of boatmen squat above the riverbank, two gentlemen gaze up at the tree from which Jwala Pershad and Gungu Mehtar, among many others, were hanged. Just behind them, on the Hardeo Temple's ledge, is the now missing memorial cross. Standing further right on the upper bank is a sombre circle of British men and women, probably hearing an account of the massacre. Similar to the vessels Nana Sahib provided, an excursion boat furnished with English dining chairs awaits its passengers, moored beside the plinth on which Nana's courtiers oversaw the attack. Further in the foreground two Indian women evoke the ayahs who watched their memsahibs' families massacred. And in the far distance, beyond the boat and a peddler's skiff, is the iron bridge that replaced the Bridge of Boats that British forces traversed on their marches into Awadh. Author's collection.

Sati Chaura Ghat and Hardeo Temple in dry weather, as seen from a sandbar. Author's collection.

When the officers returned to the Entrenchment, they found that the garrison's joy had dissipated, diluted now by deferred grief and growing foreboding. Groups of men, women and children had followed the trail to the sepulchral well to say prayers over the common grave of their comrades, friends and loved ones, covering their mouths as they approached, disturbing the flies with the notes and mementoes they dropped over the rim.

Entangled to a depth of sixty feet were the corpses of sergeants and corporals and privates, gunners and bombardiers, drummers and fifers and buglers—democratically intertwined with their officers, boxwallas, civil servants, Eurasians, railwaymen, women and children.

Still more corpses were tipped into the well that day. Exhausted by his ravings, a Reverend Haycock succumbed in the arms of his wounded and elderly mother. Captain Jenkins died 'in excruciating agony' from a wound to the jaw. Others lay comatose and too critically wounded to be moved.

As news of the capitulation circulated, servants approached the Entrenchment to inquire after their employers. They bore worrisome tidings. Thomas Greenway's servant, Kalka Pershad, agreed to go into the city and obtain 300 rupees from the mahajans (moneylenders), but told his master that he had heard that the rebels intended to massacre the sahibs at the river. The garrison's forebodings deepened as Nana's gunners arrived to haul away the Entrenchment's batteries. Not that the guns were much use: only two were still capable of firing even Lieutenant Delafosse's improvised charges. But the garrison was disturbed by the presence of the same gunners whose merciless barrage had killed so many of their loved ones. And with the gunners came a party of sowars with a string of carts into which Nana's coolies loaded up what remained of the garrison's treasure of about 120,000 rupees, though for the time being they left untouched what remained of the stores and ammunition.

Nana had hoped to get the flotilla under way that night, but he had been unable to assemble enough palanquins and bearers for the women, children and wounded. He announced now that the garrison would have to delay its departure until morning.

The delay made Wheeler uneasy, and, either voluntarily or at the General's insistence, Nana Sahib designated no less a personage than his Brigadier, Jwala Pershad, and two other functionaries to act as hostages: guarantors that the rebels would not attack the Entrenchment in the night.

As the great orange sun descended and a slight breeze stirred across the Entrenchment yard, soldiers shared their rations of rum with each other and handed around secret caches of food. A few contrived to entertain the children by beating time on casks with sticks and dancing dusty, cadaverous jigs.

Jwala Pershad had promised Wheeler that he would personally see to it that no harm would come to the garrison in the morning, but when, late in the evening, a rifle fired from the southernmost outer barrack, the rebel batteries suddenly opened up.

No doubt with an outraged officer's sabre at his throat, Pershad gained permission to send one of his companions off, and after a few more volleys the firing ceased. Once their initial panic ebbed away, some in the garrison may have been reassured by this episode. The garrison was virtually defenceless, and yet the rebels had ceased their firing. Surely if they intended to massacre everyone, they would have done so that night.

27 June
The Departure

After a fitful night's sleep, many of the women rose before dawn to light the heaps of splinters their children had collected and bake chapattis for the journey. Here and there they helped one another improvise and secure their ragged clothing.

The garrison's transport arrived an hour or more later, advancing towards Ashe's battery and into the first light as the sun cleared the Ganga Cliff. Sixteen commissariat elephants the rebels had captured led the way, followed by perhaps eighty palanquins and an assortment of horse and bullock carts.

Fanning out to either side of this caravan was a multitude of local people—some would claim they numbered in the thousands. At the sight of them approaching in the whirling dust, people tucked last-minute mementoes into their clothing. A few servants entered the Entrenchment looking for their employers. One arrived to deliver his master's dog, which he had protected in his hut. Colonel Williams's servant would testify that he found his widow and her daughters 'in a wretched plight: scorched and blistered by the sun'. Despite a wound to her upper lip, Mrs Williams asked about the property left in the house, and inquired about all the servants.

Without ceremony, the garrison lifted their baggage into carts and helped the sick and wounded into their palanquins, as thousands of rebels swarmed into the Entrenchment until 'there was hardly any place to stand'.

The treatment the officers received seemed to depend in part on their regiment. In one corner of the yard sepoys of the 53rd meekly sought out officers like Thomson and Delafosse to commiserate over their sufferings. Thomson, in turn, asked one of his native officers how many mutineers had been killed laying siege to the Entrenchment. Expecting it to be a thousand, he was disappointed to hear it had been more like 750.

At the head of the column, a group of Major Vibart's sowars helped his wife and their two surviving children into their palanquin and, according to Mowbray Thomson, escorted them out of the Entrenchment 'with the most profuse demonstrations of respect'.

Deserted, picked over by scavengers, Wheeler's Entrenchment was the most desolate of all the sites associated with the uprising. Author's collection.

Elsewhere, however, some mutineers made a point of brushing past their former commanders without saluting. 'Come to the boats. All is ready,' they commanded, pointing towards the river with their drawn tulwars.

General Wheeler's own elephant had been brought for him and his family, and Lady Wheeler and her daughters climbed into its howdah for the ride to the ghat. But perhaps choosing not to be restricted to such a ponderous beast, the old General elected to ride a horse. Climbing onto a skinny galloway, he was heard to mutter that he had been duped again.

Nana Sahib's mahouts (elephant drivers) refused to command their beasts to sit on the ground to receive their passengers. Mrs Cook, Amy's pregnant and shell-shocked mother, tried to board by pulling herself up by its tail but lost her hold and fell heavily. Some of the wounded also slipped off, landing excruciatingly on their wounded limbs. Thus, the hackeries, ox carts and shaded palanquins became the vehicles of choice. Some were loaded with baggage and sent ahead, but so many officers and their vestigial families laid claim to the palanquins that Moore had to leave behind eleven wounded men with a promise to fetch them when the rest of the garrison had reached the river.

Many women climbed into hackeries, but everyone else, including Jonah's family, had to proceed on foot. Nevertheless, the garrison slowly arranged itself into a kind of funnel shape with Wheeler at the head and the others spread out, as ragtag as camp followers, waiting to enter the procession as it stretched down the road towards the river.

At about eight o'clock a sowar galloped up to convey Nana's apologies. His Highness's underlings had evidently underestimated the extent of the garrison's baggage. If the coolies were to load any more onto the boats there would not be enough room left for the evacuees; Nana would have to send the rest along in a separate flotilla. For the same reason, none of the garrison's servants would be permitted to accompany them to Allahabad.

As the sepoys pulled the ayahs and assorted servants out of the column, the children began to cry. Jonah's ayah would describe how his long-suffering daughter Polly kept 'calling to her all the while, until she was hid from her view'.

Promising a thousand rupees to each of his servants should he survive the embarkation, and absently handing a sack of money to the Greenways' elderly ayah, Wheeler ordered, 'Quick march', and led what was left of the garrison to the river, leaving the Entrenchment in rebel hands.

27 June
The March to Sati Chaura

'Never, surely,' wrote Lieutenant Mowbray Thomson, 'was there such an emaciated, ghostly party of human beings as we.' Women who 'had once been beautiful' had been 'stripped of every personal charm, some with, some without gowns; fragments of finery were made available no longer for decoration, but decorum'. His fellow officers' uniforms were 'rent and wretched, and with nondescript mixtures of apparel, more or less insufficient in all'.

Alarmed by the size and temper of the crowd, Moore rode ahead to instruct the officers not to wait for the whole garrison to board; each party must push off as soon as their boats were loaded and make for the other side of the river.

Nevertheless, there was a certain 'order of progress' to the line of march along what their countrymen would later call 'the Via Dolorosa of the Empire'. At least two senior officers—Williamson and Wiggen—proceeded up front with the Wheelers and Emily Vibart and her children, thus adhering to the same protocols that had obtained in ballrooms and banquet halls and, outlandishly, the Entrenchment itself. Major Vibart was the last to ride out of the Entrenchment, but apparently caught up with his family at the head of the column.

Water buffalo pause along the nullah (ravine) that the garrison followed to the Ganga. The route to Sati Chowra has remained more or less as it was in 1857. Photograph by P.G.O. Taylor.

The heat was already asserting itself. By this hour, in another life, the ladies would have been returning from their morning rides to take breakfast on their verandahs or in their cool and shuttered rooms. Riding an elephant, Amy and her family could see the extent of the crowd, the rubble of the bungalows neighbouring St. John's and the rebel pickets' abandoned stations along the drainage ditch. But the passengers swaying low to the ground in their palanquins could see only the legs of the sowars' ponies and the faces of the soldiers marching alongside and the curiosity-seekers who lined the route to bid the feringhee good riddance.

The sick and wounded women lying in their soiled bandages and torn clothes slid the palanquins' shutters closed against the crowd's stares. Others staggered down the middle of the road, many of them barefoot, their clothes patched and pinched together with string and pins as they jollied their children along. A few soldiers carried cases and bundles on their heads like coolies, others feebly marched like pensioners on parade.

Some sahibs tried to resist the troopers as they yanked away the loyal servants who tried to remain with their employers, and 'a great disturbance was the consequence'. Here and there mutineers took hold of former regimental comrades who had stuck by their commanders. About 300 yards from the Entrenchment, in the middle of the column, a group of mutineers from the 56th took hold of their old Jemadar Khoda Bux and roughed him up, grabbing his musket and cartridge box, knocking away his turban and stripping off his uniform before finally dragging him and his son towards their regiment's old lines. Over the protests of Lieutenant Goad, the rebels dragged off four other sepoys as well, including Govind Singh, whom the Lieutenant had been leading by the hand.

Palanquin bearers paused from time to time to shift their burdens, and here and there a family called out pleas and instructions to the few friendly and familiar faces in the crowd. The result was that the column gradually stretched out for almost half a mile, with the crowd closing around a few stray groups and shuffling along with them towards the river.

The front of the column was apparently greeted with a measure of awe. The senior officers and the stately elephants and the Vibarts' sowar escort caused the crowd to back away, some reflexively bowing and salaaming. Indeed, from his vantage in front of the procession, Delafosse concluded that the entire garrison was proceeding 'without being molested in the least'.

But the evacuees marched in a kind of declension, with the crippled and destitute tending towards the rear, so that the garrison appeared to the crowd ever more helpless and degraded. As this spectral parade faltered past, the crowd grew bolder.

Amy Horne watched in horror as the sickly Captain Kempland of the 56th Native Infantry was 'severely beaten' by a group of his sepoys until they managed to yank his musket from him; according to Amy, 'many other officers were treated in the same way', including the prostrate Colonel John Ewart and his wife, whose sepoys diverted their palanquin and hacked them to death.

The Greenways' elderly ayah stumbled after the garrison, carrying the sack of rupees Wheeler had given her, when a sepoy grabbed it from her, struck her in the back with his tulwar, and left her for dead.

Jonah would be told how townspeople rummaged through the Entrenchment, 'inspecting every mite of ground in search of spoil.' One of them even turned up a pocket watch Thomson had buried in the outer barracks. A group of insurgents ducked into the Main Guard and emerged dragging the eleven wounded Europeans by their bedding, tumbling them into the middle of the yard where young men knocked them about until sepoys killed them with their muskets.

A mile away, Wheeler and Moore reached the high road that ran along the top of the Ganga Cliff and turned south along the river. It hardly seemed possible, but hundreds more onlookers now came into view, rushing for vantage points along the late Colonel Williams's compound walls.

Wheeler crossed the whitewashed bridge over the nullah and turned down towards the water. Some of the villagers in the crowd carried weapons—swords, spears, axes—but they did not brandish them as Wheeler stopped his galloway and dismounted to join his wife and daughters on their elephant. As sowars rode ahead of the column, commanding everyone to stand back and not follow the garrison down to the ghat, the crowd made way.

Riding behind the sowars, Captains Moore and Turner posted down to the water to inspect the boats, only to find that either the river had receded in the night or the boats had been hauled closer to shore, for they now sat in a mere two feet of water, their hulls plumped down in the sand.

27 June
Sati Chaura

On the southernmost terrace of the Hardeo Temple, a group of well-dressed Indian gentlemen were seated on mats. Azimullah, every trace of western clothing discarded now for the immaculate white kurtha pyjama of a pious Moslem nobleman, salaamed as Wheeler's officers passed. Nana's courtiers sat nearby: Jwala Pershad, the bespectacled Baba Bhutt and the tall, broken-nosed Bala Rao. Perhaps half a dozen others sat among them, but Nana Sahib had decided to sit the embarkation out at Savada House. By some unconfirmed accounts, it was the stout, vigilant Tatya Tope, Nana's boyhood instructor in the Maratha arts of war, who seemed to be overseeing the embarkation.

As soon as the first of Wheeler's party reached the river, they hurried out of their hackeries and palanquins, and dashed and staggered for the water. Lady Wheeler and her two daughters slid down from their elephant and into the lead boat, with the General himself following after them, accompanied, apparently in defiance of the sowars, by several of his servants. Joining the Wheelers were Wiggen, Williamson and Captain Whiting, as though the boat had been reserved, oddly enough, for Ws.

A sadhu sits on the terrace once occupied by Nana Sahib's courtiers, as they oversaw the operation at the river. Very little has changed at this site, and even though this upriver view was photographed well after the uprising, it shows the kinds of shallows and sandbars that the fleeing garrison had to navigate. Courtesy of Zoe Yalland.

The other boats filled up according to rank and race, but each was provided with a guard of at least two European soldiers or junior officers to help the boatmen heave their hulls out of the sand and into the current. In one boat far upstream from Wheeler's flagship, Eurasian musicians and their families joined perhaps a score of girls from the Free School and a couple of European soldiers.

Keeping an eye on the gathering crowd along the rim of the embankment, the soldiers and officers desperately heaved the women and children and the wounded into the boats as fast as they could, as mutineers taunted them.

'We found that the boats were not very close to the shore,' wrote Amy, and there were no gangways. 'We had to wade knee-deep through the water, and it was pitiful to witness the difficulty of the aged, the sick and the wounded in clambering up the boats' sides.' Her stepfather John Cook and his two sons and two daughters settled under their boat's thatch while Amy and two soldiers sat on the bamboo foredeck with Amy's injured half-sister. But in all the confusion, her mother had been conveyed to a different boat.

As many as fifteen men, women and children piled into each vessel, crowding their jittery crews and grinding the hulls ever deeper into the Ganga's sandy bottom. In some of the boats the ladies were pleased to find that the crews had thoughtfully lit cooking fires in their little brick stoves. But much of the food Turner had watched the coolies load onto the boats had disappeared overnight. Some of the boats still had no bamboo floors, others lacked oars and ropes.

This etching from Thomson's account gives some sense of the scene at Sati Chaura as the garrison embarked, including elephants, ayahs conveying children to the river, a vast mob on the riverbank, a mounted sowar overseeing the operation, an officer trying to heave a pregnant woman into a boat, and a palanquin set in the sand. Author's collection.

Limping from the wound in his thigh, Mowbray Thomson boarded a boat somewhere near the front of the line while his comrade Henry Delafosse climbed into the lead boat and, laying down his musket and discarding his coat, began to work one of the bamboo pilings out of the sand to pole the vessel into the stream. A few officers apparently rode down the line of boats, directing the embarkation as best they could. But soon all of the boats were full and a great many of the evacuees were still wading along the shore, stumbling down the nullah or crossing the wooden bridge hundreds of yards away.

If any officer approached Nana Sahib's men to demand more boats, none were apparently willing to wait to see them provided. The tattered survivors of three weeks' siege continued to scramble aboard boats already 'crowded to suffocation', or desperately splashed upstream, begging for berths in Goordial's bobbing fleet. Major Vibart joined Emily and his two surviving children in the lead boat, and no sooner had he stepped onto the bamboo deck than someone gave the order to push off.

Wheeler's elephant may have given the general's boat a nudge as Delafosse and his comrades poled the boat away from shore. Some said Wheeler had bribed his boatmen with 1,000 rupees to free the boat, but Thomson believed it was simply of lighter drought than the others. In any case, the vessel began to work its way free of the shallows.

This sudden motion seemed to agitate the sixteen sowars who had escorted Major Vibart to the river with such solicitude. Two now galloped up the nullah, shouting to the crowd to disperse, while another suddenly commanded all the boats' crews to come up to receive their pay.

In the far distance west of the river three guns manned by sepoys of the 17th BNI opened fire, and all along the riverbank boatmen hurled their oars into the water and leaped into the shallows. The officers on board the boats gaped a moment as the boatmen landed with a series of splashes and squattered towards the river bank. Men, women and children stranded at the water's edge froze in confusion and then pointed in horror at the dense, green-grey smoke billowing from several of the vessels' roofs, where boatmen had secreted embers from their cooking fires in the sun-parched thatch.

In J.R. Skelton's fastidious imagining of the attack at Sati Chaura, the boatmen have fled, the thatch roofs are ablaze, and British soldiers are desperately trying to heave their crowded boats into deep water.
Author's collection.

Before most of the boatmen had reached the riverbank, a bugle sounded and three more cannon boomed nearby. One fired from the heights of Henry Christie's compound, spraying the shoal with grape. The others sent cannon balls arcing from the tall grass on the Lucknow side and plunging into the river, splashing the flotilla with water and mud.

As the cannon fire echoed from bank to bank across the Ganga's chop, the little band of sowars opened fire with their carbines and rode off, making way for the seemingly impossible number of sepoys who now swarmed out from between the village of Sati Chaura and Henry Christie's compound wall, running the 100 yards towards Hardeo Temple and firing their muskets. A second squad emerged from the fleeing crowd along the nullah, some skidding down the riverbank's slope to take positions behind bushes and heaps of timber, others firing a round up towards the stragglers at the bridge. And 100 yards downriver yet another party of mutineers began to funnel out from behind the southern wall of Colonel Williams's compound, where a team of gunners were hauling a fourth cannon into position.

The two soldiers on Amy's boat fell wounded in the first volley of musket fire and slumped off the roof and into the hull, leaving Amy and her injured sister 'stupefied with terror and amazement'. Men desperately struck at the smouldering thatch with their discarded coats, cut with their sabres at the moorings, grabbed spars to pole the hulls free, ordered the women and children down, reached for their muskets on the bamboo decks. From some boats enraged officers and soldiers shot a gratuitous round at the retreating boatmen, while others fired at the gathering sepoys, sending two toppling back onto the sand.

This A.D. McCormick illustration for The Romance of Empire: India, *vividly captures the chaos in the shallows as the rebel fire intensified.* Author's collection.

The sepoys arrayed themselves in no particular order, but laid a tremendous fire; the first round from north of the temple killed over a dozen evacuees. Soon the rebel gunners found their range and nine-pound shot crashed into the frail old hulls.

By now many of the thatched roofs had burst into furious flames, stoked by the hot wind that rushed unobstructed down the Ganga's course. Fires consumed the bamboo decks and roiled into the hulls, igniting the clothing and bedding of the sick and injured. Their frenzied screams momentarily pierced the din. 'The flames were terrifically fierce,' Thomson recalled, 'and their intense sufferings were not protracted.'

In this reoriented and colourized illustration, flames engulf two of the lead boats as rebel gunfire picks off the stragglers. Author's collection.

It was Jonah's belief that his wife Ellen and his daughter Polly, his brother and sister, and the rest of their family were among those consumed by the flames. But some women and children, their hair and clothing ablaze, managed to tumble blindly over the sides of their boat and into the water. Many who landed in the shallows on the

Kanpur side were cut down by the sepoys' fusillade. But others who jumped off the opposite side found refuge from the sepoys' muskets behind the hulls or, 'calling on God for help', waded far enough out into the river to expose only their heads to the rebel fire. But many of them drowned, and even those who stayed afloat were vulnerable to the grape fired from the guns on the opposite shore.

Some boats escaped the flames but could not be budged. Though the water was still too shallow to float the hulls, it was deep enough to consume the children whose mothers had pitched them overboard, and ladies desperately scrambled through the water and the smoke, feeling in the dun of the shallows for their drowning children.

Somehow, in all this lethal chaos, Thomson had managed to escape to Wheeler's receding boat. He was just one in a general exodus of able-bodied men; to Henry Delafosse it appeared that the men of the garrison had 'rushed to the first boat they saw loose'. Perhaps a dozen swam with Thomson, 'beating the water for life'. Another group paddled straight across the river, trying to reach the far shore, but most of these were killed by rounds of grape or picked off by the sepoys of the 17th BNI from Sultanpur, who now emerged from the grass along the Lucknow side of the river, firing their muskets.

In the meantime, a second boat had reeled out of the shoal and into the stream, only to be struck below the water line by round shot. The surviving able-bodied passengers jumped out and clambered into Wheeler's boat. Two companies of sepoys ran along the embankment, following the lone boat's agonizing progress down the river. In the sepoys' undiscriminating musket fire officers who had cheated death for three weeks of bombardment began to fall. As others tried to keep up a covering fire, young officers leaped into the water to try to heave the boat out of range, but one after another they were all shot down, including Captain Moore.

When the rebels finally stormed the boat, Lady Wheeler and her daughters jumped overboard, but she and Eliza apparently drowned, and only Margaret Wheeler, their youngest, made it to the riverbank.

Still hiding in what remained of her vessel, Amy huddled with her sister, whispering prayers. Suddenly the boat tipped violently as sepoys climbed up over the side. As they made their way towards Amy and her sister, they killed several children cowering in the hold. A sepoy grabbed Amy by the arm and commanded her to hand over 'all I possessed'. She gave up 'a few trinkets', but the sepoys ran their hands through her gown, searching for more.

A sowar riding saddle-deep in the water came up alongside and commanded her to come to him. When she turned away, he ordered one of the sepoys to throw her over the side. In the struggle, Amy lost hold of Florence, and as she was thrown into the river, she could hear her little sister cry, 'Oh, Amy, don't leave me!'

Haunted ever after by her sister's cries, she stripped off her gown and managed to stay afloat long enough to reach the bank.

In this portrait little Florence Cook clings to her half-sister Amy Horne, as she would when they cowered together in one of the burning boats at Sati Chaura. Collection of Andrew Ward, courtesy of Lucy Kallebring.

In this fanciful depiction of the attack, a few boats push out into the stream while others stuck in the mud are destroyed by fire. The two figures in the foreground are supposed to be Nana Sahib and Tatya Tope. In this artist's imagination, Kanpur is a vast Hindu metropolis, but downstream from Sati Chaura the only buildings in view would have been the charred remains of the cantonment's bungalows. Author's collection.

All this had transpired in less than an hour. At around ten o'clock a messenger rushed down the nullah and handed a note to Tatya

Tope, reportedly from Nana Sahib commanding that the killing cease. A bugle sounded a ceasefire, whereupon the sowars and sepoys stopped attacking the survivors and began to drag and prod them up the bank.

All the men lying in the shallows were either dead or near dead. About 120 women and children were assembled on the riverbank, some of them wounded, all of them soaked in mud and blood.

After half an hour the women were ordered to their feet, but many could hardly walk. So, the sepoys piled them back into the same hackeries that had carried them to the river. By this time the townspeople the mutineers had shooed away began to return from their hiding places to watch as the women and children proceeded up the nullah and across the parade ground to Savada House. The sight of them rendered many onlookers speechless. Some sepoys expressed remorse, declaring that it had been 'a crime to put to the sword such fair and tender creatures'. Emerging from his tent, Nana Sahib ordered that they all be brought into the main hall under his own Maratha guard.

27 June
Amy Horne

In all the mayhem that morning, Amy Horne had crawled up the embankment and hidden in the brush. Chanting prayers, she fell into 'a sort of drowsy fit' from which she was soon wakened by footsteps. Amy jumped to her feet to find not an approaching rebel but Margaret Wheeler, the General's daughter, who had been hiding in the shallows nearby.

Amy and Margaret were too terrified to be of much comfort to each other, but they cowered together in the bushes for an hour until a rebel party stumbled upon them. A mounted sowar apparently hauled Margaret up behind him and rode off with her into the countryside, while the others led Amy away. Crowds of onlookers threatened to kill her, but an African eunuch from Lucknow covered her near-nakedness with a sheet, helped her to her feet, and led her to a tent, where he guarded her as she slept.

27 June
Nana Sahib

That evening, Nana Sahib issued a proclamation declaring that 'by the grace of God, and the destroying fortune of the King', all of 'the white faces' who had opposed him had 'entered hell'.

The rebels held a grand review on the plain north-east of Savada House. By now his army consisted not only of the four resident Kanpur regiments but the 12th and 13th Native Infantry, four regiments of irregular cavalry, companies from the 17th BNI, detachments of sepoys from Fatehgarh and Allahabad, the 2nd Oudh Irregular Infantry, plus artillery batteries, a regiment's worth of newly recruited Kanpur militia, and a 'great mob' of matchlock-men led by local taluqdars.

Nana Sahib urged the people of the city to 'celebrate this victory with rejoicings and peals of artillery' and that night the soldiers' camps were illuminated by mustard-oil lamps. As troops assembled in their thousands, Nana Sahib Peshwa Bahadur finally received the twenty-one-gun salute that the British had denied his adoptive father some forty years ago. The cannon barrels glowed red hot in a positive orgy of salutes. Nineteen guns were fired for Bala Rao, his brother and Governor-General, and seventeen for Brigadier Jwala Pershad. Heaping praises on his ministers for 'the way in which he got possession of the Entrenchment', he extolled Azimullah and Pershad for planning 'so easy a conquest' at Sati Chaura and avenging Neill's victims.

28–30 June
On the Ganga

All the next day, Wheeler and his dwindling party heaved their way downstream. In the middle of the night clouds came roiling down the river, unleashing a torrent of rain, and the fugitives awoke to find their boat floating freely down the rising Ganga. 'Some fresh hopes buoyed us up again; but daylight returned to reveal the painful fact that we had drifted out of the navigable channel into a siding of the river,' and as the boat ground to a groaning halt on yet another sandbar, thirty or forty rebels resumed their fire.

By 9 a.m. on the 29th, Major Vibart decided that their only hope was for a party of able-bodied men to charge directly into them, thus drawing their fire as the rest dropped into the water to push the boat free. It seemed 'a forlorn enterprise', but Vibart invested eleven able-bodied soldiers in it, under the command of Lieutenants Thomson and Delafosse and Sergeant Grady of the 84th.

The lead officers' boat struggles down the Ganga as sepoys fire from the bank. The original illustration has been flipped horizontally to correct the boat's orientation with the riverbank. Author's collection.

If Thomson was any measure, 'able-bodied' had become a relative term, for he had been thrice wounded by this time, with grapeshot in his thigh, a bullet in his back and a gash on his head where a sniper's bullet had grazed him only the day before. But, as Delafosse put it, 'there was nothing left but to charge [the sepoys] and drive them away', and with a few whispered prayers the men huddled down in the hold for a moment, readying their muskets, and then emerged with a roar, tumbling down into the shallows and, 'maddened by desperation', rushing the sepoys on the shore.

At first, the startled sepoys fell back in confusion, but as Thomson and Delafosse led their men further up the embankment, other rebels closed behind them, 'until we were thoroughly surrounded by a mingled party of natives, armed and unarmed'. The squad splashed down into the shallows downstream from where they had left the boat. But they saw no trace of it. Giving up on ever seeing 'either the boat or our doomed companions anymore', they fled into the countryside 'with a rabble of ryots and sepoys at our heels'.

Apparently, shortly after Thomson and his party charged the rebels, more and more sepoys assembled along the embankment, firing their muskets at Wheeler's boat. It is possible it had managed to float a few more yards downstream, but by now the combination of musket and artillery fire was so intense that Major Vibart raised a white flag, and a body of sepoys waded out into the shallows to accept their surrender and collect their arms.

The rebels assembled carts from a nearby village to transport the women and children. Apparently, some of the rebels' ferocity had been spent, for they did not handle the women as roughly as they had two days before, nor search them, nor bind them, nor take away their valuables.

In the meantime, Thomson and his detachment fled barefoot for three miles, trying to elude their pursuers over rugged ravines.

By and by, they all ducked into a small Hindu temple except for Sergeant Grady, who toppled forward by the door with a bullet in his brain. Thomson ordered four men to kneel down in the temple's single narrow entrance with their bayonets fixed while the rest stood in the deafening dark, firing into the crowd. The rebels charged with such violence that several of them were pushed against the fugitives' bayonets and killed, until their piled bodies provided Thomson's men with cover.

The flight from the temple, from Mowbray Thomson's The Story of Cawnpore. Author's collection.

At last, the rebels decided to smoke the British out by heaping brush near the door and setting it ablaze. But apparently the wind changed and carried the smoke away from the door. Undeterred, several sepoys hurled sacks of gunpowder into the 'red-hot ashes', forcing Thomson and his men to flee. Six of them fell, but the rest managed to hurl themselves and their muskets into the river.

The weight of their ammunition pouches dragged them under, but 'while we were thus submerged, we escaped the first volley that they fired'. Removing their pouches, they bobbed back to the surface and furiously swam away, so that by the time most of the rebels had reloaded 'there were only heads for them to aim at'.

On the left half of this illustration from Mowbray Thomson's The Story of Cawnpore, *the uniformed figures firing on the five swimmers are sepoys, though by this time they probably would have discarded their uniforms and donned civilian clothes. The figures on the right cheering on the sepoys from a sandbar are villagers.* Author's collection.

Nevertheless, the rebels managed to hit two of these heads in the second volley, reducing Thomson's band to five. As they paddled downstream Delafosse and a private named Murphy were lured to a sandbar near the opposite shore, where two villagers promised them protection. But the two Britons balked, whereupon the villagers attacked them with clubs as they swam for their lives back into deep water. They had better luck than Private Ryan, who, swimming on his back, blundered onto the same sandbar and was bludgeoned to death.

Now all that was left of the band were Thomson, Delafosse, Privates Murphy of the 84th and Sullivan of the 1st Madras Fusiliers. Divesting themselves of their clothing, for two or three hours these four somehow managed to stay afloat and out of range. At last, their pursuers dwindled down to a single sowar who watched from his horse as they drifted away. Once safely out of sight, the four fugitives—the only British men to survive the attack at Sati Chaura Ghat—crept into the shallows to rest, sitting in the wet sand with the water up to their necks and startling a trio of benign, long-nosed crocodiles that had been basking nearby.

Fortunately, they had floated into the domain of the elderly loyalist Raja Digbijai Singh of Balrampur, head of the most powerful Rajput clan in the district, whose warriors turned up to rescue them. Plied with sweetmeats and offered piles of straw and carpets, the four exhausted men bedded down for the night.

Loyalist Rajput matchlock-men similar to the party that rescued Thomson, Delafosse, Murphy and Sullivan. Collection of the New York Public Library.

As Thomson lay on his pallet, replaying the horrors and terrors of the past few days, he kept returning to the same 'ludicrous' note of self-congratulation: 'How excellent an investment that guinea had proved,' he kept telling himself, 'which I spent a year or two before at the baths in Holborn, learning to swim!'

Painted by Lieutenant C.W. Crump of the Madras Artillery, no image better expresses the desolation with which the British received the news of the massacres at Kanpur than this bleak view of the Entrenchment from behind the insurgents' former lines, where a stork ponders a rebel's bones.
Courtesy of Mark Probett.

30 June
Allahabad

On 30 June, Henry Havelock had arrived with his column at Allahabad to find Neill ailing and his column exhausted from three weeks of burning houses, hanging suspected rebels, and chasing off the farmers and contractors Havelock would need to equip and supply his troops. In the meantime, Company magistrates in

Benares had continued to hang scores of local people, while squads of Highlanders rampaged through the surrounding countryside.

In one village 2,000 peasants and rebels united to avenge the Highlanders' atrocities, but the 78th surrounded them and set fire to the village, shooting anyone who came running out of the flames. Recovering from sunstroke and frustrated by the delays arising from his own retributive policies, Neill sent Major Sydenham Renaud with a force of 300 Europeans and 400 Sikhs to pacify the Grand Trunk Road.

The means Neill proposed to Renaud were monstrous: all villages were to be destroyed, all males executed, and any sepoys 'not giving a good account of themselves' were to be hanged.

Renaud's Highlanders bed down for the night after a hard day festooning the trees along the Grand Trunk Road with Indian men accused of siding with the rebels. John Company had already refined their technique a year before, putting down a rebellion by displaced Santhal tribesmen.
Author's collection.

So far, Calcutta had received nothing but bad news from the Bengal Presidency. The reports of mutinies at Meerut, Delhi, Agra and Kanpur had been followed by accounts of uprisings in Jhansi, Gwalior, Banda, Bundelkhand and Rohilkhand, in most of which great numbers of Europeans had been killed.

Reports from the Punjab predicted that the Company's primarily Sikh army would soon mutiny, and the news from down the country was equally worrisome. The Bombay and Madras armies had held firm, but how long could they be expected to remain loyal if the Bengal mutineers succeeded? The Marathas in the Western Ghats were expected to break out at any hour and join the Rani of Jhansi and their reborn Peshwa, Nana Sahib, against the British. Even the loyal Nizam of Hyderabad was said to be faltering. A few more British defeats and the Company's rule could entirely unravel.

Rumours of the fall of Kanpur reached Havelock almost as soon as he arrived in Allahabad, but he dismissed them until 2 July, when two Indian couriers claimed to have 'passed through Kanpur and [seen] Wheeler's force destroyed'. Perhaps out of guilt that he had not proceeded earlier, Neill refused to believe it, and accused Havelock of losing his nerve.

Two days passed before Havelock and his army finally lumbered out of Allahabad. By now he and Neill were hardly speaking to each other, and bickered over how many men should march with Havelock and how many should remain behind with Neill.

The Illustrated London News *imagined the sun breaking through the clouds as Havelock's relief force departed from Allahabad.* Author's collection.

Havelock's army had been hastily assembled. It included detachments of Her Majesty's 84th, whose comrades had fallen at Kanpur, the 1st Madras Fusiliers, the 78th Highlanders Havelock had recently commanded in Persia, a battery of Royal Artillery and 150 Ferozepore Sikhs who would eventually prove as brave—and as atrocious—as their British comrades-in-arms. These were supplemented by a miscellany of British volunteers who had stepped forward at Benares and Allahabad. In addition to the usual crapulous and semi-suicidal deserters Havelock's officers dragged out of the grog shops and flophouses of Calcutta, the ranks of the Fusiliers had been swollen by teenaged Eurasians recruited from the Madras Military Orphanage.

Aside from the sepoys whose privileges—including immunity from flogging—the British troops bitterly resented, the only Indians they knew well were mostly the lowest sort: camp followers, usurers, whores. Calling themselves the 'God-forgotten', they regarded their service in India as a kind of perdition. They might exact revenge, reassert Company authority and join in Havelock's prayers. But they also saw this expedition as a chance to pay India back for cramped barracks, bastard children, filthy bazaars, sunstroke, fever and venereal disease.

As Havelock departed with his army for Kanpur, the inhabitants of Allahabad scowled at them from the roofs of their remaining houses. No sooner had they cleared the outskirts of the city than a tropical rain turned the tramped road into a quagmire and doubled the weight of the folded tents lagging behind them in bullock carts. By the time they encamped that night, the column had managed only eight miles.

As they marched on the next morning, the sun illuminated the nightmare landscape Renaud had left in his bloody wake. Havelock shelled several reputedly rebel villages along the way, and apparently executed a few suspected spies, but his exhausted men generally ignored the peasants who dared show their faces.

30 June
Savada House

On the morning of 30 June, the survivors from Wheeler's boat were escorted to Savada House, where Nana Sahib emerged from his tent to congratulate their captors and condemn the men to death.

No one knows for sure, but among these captives may have been Wheeler himself. By one account, he had already been beheaded on the 27th while boarding his boat, and a sepoy was later hanged on the charge of having done the deed. But it is more likely Hamlah was still alivc, if barely, when Nana ordered that the officers be executed.

According to one account, the sepoys refused, out of respect for Wheeler. But as the women and children listened in the gloom of Savada House, less nostalgic rebels led all seventeen officers out onto the parade ground, shot them down, and arranged for their corpses to be carted back to the Ganga in trussed-up bundles of five or six.

1 July
Nana Sahib

'As by the kindness of God and the good fortune of the Emperor,' Nana's heralds proclaimed through the streets of Kanpur, 'all the Christians'—in another proclamation that day they would call them 'the yellow-faced and narrow-minded people'—'who were at Delhi, Poonah, Satarah and other places, and even those 5,000 European soldiers who went in disguise into the former city were discovered, and destroyed and sent to hell by the pious and sagacious troops.'

Nana Sahib returned to his palace at Bithur, and in an evening ceremony his Brahmins applied a sacred mark upon his forehead. Baji Rao's old throne was dusted off, and to another round of artillery salutes his adopted son was formally coronated with a 'costly turban' as Srimunt Maharaj Dhiraj Nana Sahib Dhondu Pant Purdhan, Supreme Peshwa of the Maratha nation. Kanpur and Bithur were illuminated, including the sacred ghats, and children frolicked into the night with fizz-gigs and bottle rockets. Merchants sent gifts, and Nana withdrew gold from the treasury to be melted into the bangles he had promised rebel officers four weeks earlier.

And yet for the next few days Nana's actions suggested not exuberance and relief but anxiety, lassitude, even despondency. He lingered at Bithur, retreating into the quiet, upholstered interstices of his palace, ignoring his army's call to return to Kanpur. It would require the threats of his own commanders finally to convince him that the massacre at Sati Chaura had carried him inexorably into the current of his countrymen's rebellion.

2 July
Savada House

For the first three days of their imprisonment, the women and children at Savada House had been largely neglected. There were at least 180 women and children huddled together in the anteroom, encamped like tattered refugees at a train station. Many of them were wounded, few had any decent clothes; and though, after all they had endured, they constituted something of an aristocracy of the fittest, many were in shock or deranged by despair.

Whatever their ultimate fate, the surviving women and children could not remain in Savada House forever. A couple of hundred yards away a number of Nana Sahib's courtiers had moved into the Old Kanpur Hotel, where Nana had set up field headquarters. Two doors down, Jwala Pershad occupied a bungalow, and next door was another house filled, like the Assembly Rooms, with plundered British property. So, when the time came to move everyone from Savada House, it seemed sensible to install the women and children nearby.

3 July
The Bibighar

The rebels had chosen a small building known as the Bibighar, formerly the detached quarters of a British officer's mistress. At five o'clock in the afternoon of 3 July, the rebels herded the women and children down the steps of Savada House and carted them two and a half miles up the tree-lined course, across the canal, and into their new quarters.

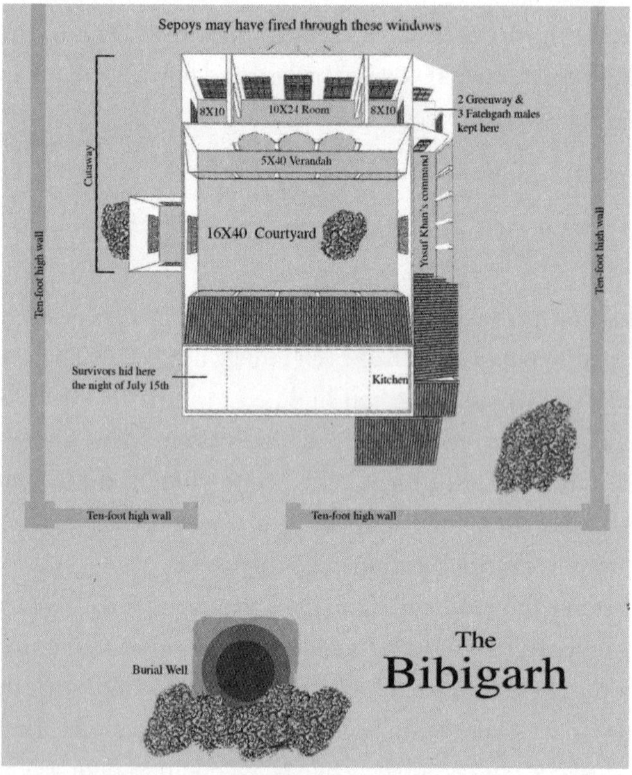

The author drew this floor plan based on various images and sources, though some are contradictory. The central mulsuri (maulsari) tree was a hardwood shade tree whose fruit and flowers were used in Ayurvedic preparations to aid in oral hygiene. Author's collection.

The house seemed ample enough for a bibi and her extended family. But by European standards the rooms were small and poorly ventilated, for the door-sized windows were shuttered closed and the walls at either end of the courtyard, combined with the surrounding compound walls, shut the Bibighar off from any breeze that might have reached it from the flow of the Ganga a quarter mile to the north-east.

Crowded together into this dismal vestige of the age of bibis and nabobs, someone had to take charge, and for the sake of their survival many of the captives probably observed some semblance of their old social hierarchy. The seniormost widows among them were disabled by wounds and, just as it had fallen to Captain Moore to keep up the defence of the Entrenchment, it may well have fallen to his widow to comfort the children and organize the ladies into rotations under the roofed verandahs, for there was not enough room for everyone to find shade at once. They subsisted on a sparse ration of dal and chapattis—though no sparser than many a ryot's diet—and soon began to succumb to infection, dysentery and cholera.

6 July
Nana Sahib

Rumours now reached Kanpur that the British had advanced some fifty miles: halfway between Allahabad and Kanpur, and were fast approaching rebel-occupied Fatehpur. To calm his army's nerves, Nana distributed the gold bangles he had promised, as well as raincoats and tents. Satisfied that he had secured the allegiance of his army, nevertheless, like Wheeler before him, he found it expedient to send some wavering sowars out of station: in this case to Delhi and Lucknow with orders 'to slay the unbelieving Nazarenes, and despatch them to hell'.

When stories circulated of an additional British relief force assembling in Calcutta, Azimullah invented a story of his own: that the Company had indeed tried to send 35,000 soldiers to India, but when they reached the Mediterranean, the Padshah of Egypt, by order of the Sultan of Turkey, had annihilated them. And as if that weren't good enough news, he was receiving reports that the Company's armies in Madras and Bombay were in open rebellion. Whether or not Kanpur's townspeople believed all this, as Tatya Tope and Jwala Pershad prepared to meet Havelock's column, many residents found it expedient to flee into the countryside.

9–10 July
Sheorajpur

Nana had already sent camel sowars eastward to scout for Havelock's force and stationed a regiment of infantry and cavalry at Sheorajpur and Bithur. On 9 July, his scouts reported that a remarkably slight British force of about 700 men was approaching, laying telegraph wire behind and perpetrating atrocities at every village they encountered.

On 10 July, a force of 3,500 men under Teeka Singh and Jwala Pershad marched out of the cantonment, confident that 'as the British force cannot be a large one, they will soon be annihilated'. Nevertheless, Nana was determined to keep the bulk of his army massed at Kanpur if they failed. The Moslems regarded this as self-serving, and accused Nana of trying merely to protect his establishment at Bithur and save his own skin.

11–12 July
The Bibighar

It was rumoured that Nana Sahib had received orders from the Emperor at Delhi to treat his prisoners decently, but more likely the conditions at the Bibighar affronted his reputation as a host. In any case, he assigned a Bengali doctor to look after the women and children, and ordered that they be supplied with fresh clothes collected from the sahibs' former dhobis (washermen).

When it became obvious that the women were languishing on their ration of dal, he hired cooks from the fish bazaar to prepare better meals, including a meat course, rum, beer and wines, and a swallow or two of milk for the children. Eventually, the prisoners were allowed to emerge from the Bibighar to sit or walk in the fresh evening air.

A few captives tried to leave some record of themselves: recording their families' histories on what paper they could scrounge from their Bibles and prayer books. But as rumours reached Nana Sahib that his prisoners' servants were smuggling messages to Havelock, Nana assigned a serving girl to take charge: a tall, fair former slave girl named Hussaini Khanum who evidently nurtured a particularly virulent hatred of British womanhood. Her first measure was to pare down the prisoners' team of bhistis (water carriers) to one. This meant that, as at the Entrenchment, there would not be enough water to bathe adequately, and in the terrible heat some of the women snipped off each other's hair against infestations of lice. There was little privacy in the courtyard: no way to shield themselves from the sight of the guards of the 6th Native Infantry who peered at them through the shutters from time to time, nor protect themselves from the prying eyes of the local people—idle boys, most of them—who used to sit along Sir George Parker's compound walls.

The Bengali doctor kept a list of the prisoners, and did what he could for the sickest women and children, apparently moving the terminal cases into a separate room from whence, after death, mehtars (members of the scavenger caste) dragged them away, stripped them of their clothes and flung them into the river.

11 July
Havelock

Apparently readers of the Illustrated London News *needed some reassurance that Havelock's men did not burn villages and hang suspected rebels without starting their day with a healthy breakfast.*
Author's collection.

Convinced by now that Kanpur had indeed fallen, Havelock proceeded in easy stages until the morning of 11 July when a rider galloped in to report that Nana's army was advancing in great strength on Renaud's camp. Havelock pushed his men on for fifteen miles, and then, after a few hours' rest, pressed on again until, to the skirl of 'The Campbells are Coming', he caught up with Renaud.

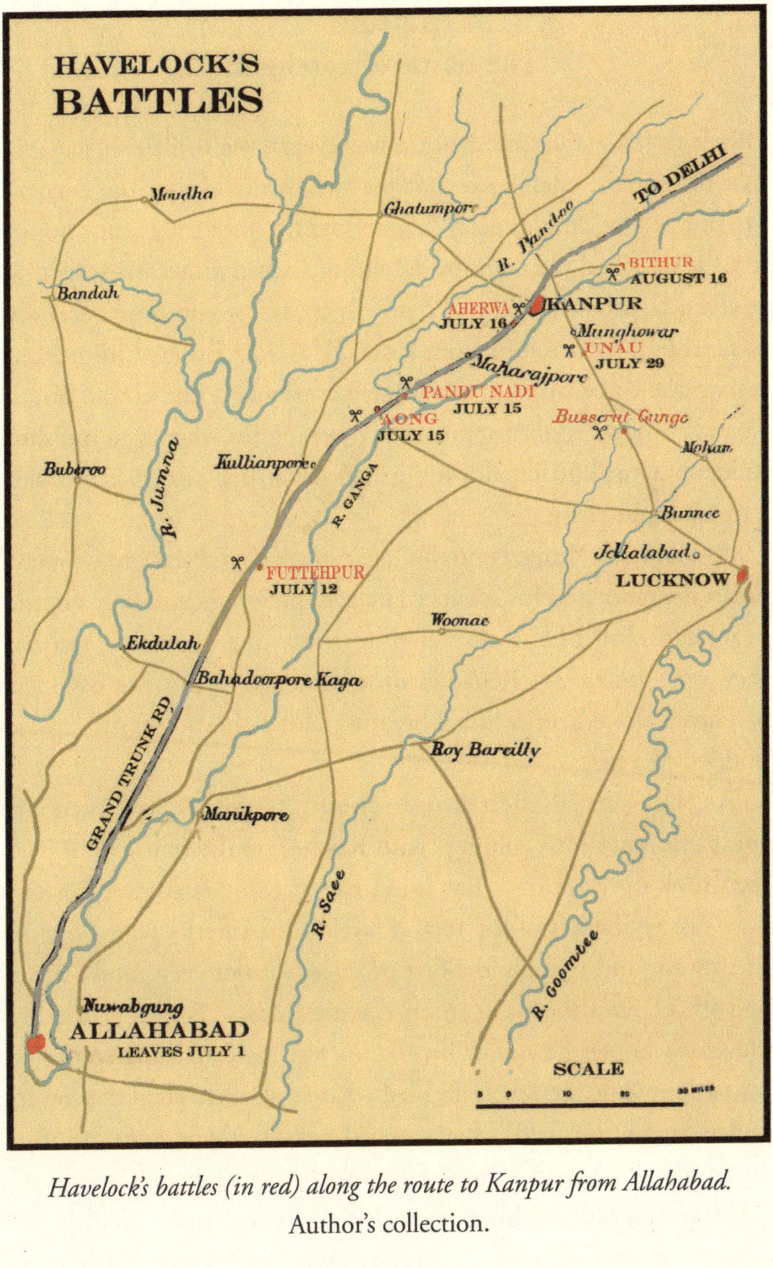

Havelock's battles (in red) along the route to Kanpur from Allahabad.
Author's collection.

12 July
The Battle of Fatehpur

Havelock knew that momentum was everything to British soldiers, that their worst enemy was not the sun or the rain or the enemy's fire but hesitation and delay. Consequently, after only a few hours' rest, he marched the combined column sixteen more miles, halting at seven in the morning of 12 July by a vast swamp four miles shy of Fatehpur. After sending out scouts, Havelock ordered his men to rest on the dry ground of a low ridge overlooking the Grand Trunk Road. He had just dismounted for morning tea when a round shot suddenly came hurtling down the road and struck a camp kettle with a tremendous clang.

As Havelock jumped onto his horse, more shot arced and bounced down the road, and his scouts came galloping back, trailing a horde of jubilant 2nd BLC sowars clad in white. But when they realized they were facing not Renaud's little detachment but the bayonets of Havelock's entire column bristling along the ridge, the sowars skidded to a halt.

As they reined their horses about, Havelock arranged his companies into four columns with Renaud on the right, while 100 men took up position a few hundred yards forward in a grove of trees just to the left of the road. Havelock's artillery opened fire on the sowars, and though 'the first practice was not very good', wrote one officer, nevertheless 'it emptied some saddles'. For a few minutes Havelock hoped he might be able to rest his exhausted troops in formation while the rebels decided what to do. But when the sowars pulled their horses aside, they revealed a vast formation of mutineers and cannon hurrying around to attack the British flank.

Havelock ordered his guns to the copse of trees to destroy the rebel batteries, and 'it was refreshing', wrote a volunteer horseman, to 'see the round shot ploughing them up, and the grape falling on all sides, and shells bursting over their heads'. Then, as a detachment on the left squattered through the 'rice swamps' to support them, his gunners hauled their artillery around to cut off the rebels' flanking movement while Renaud's Enfields poured fire on the rebels' left.

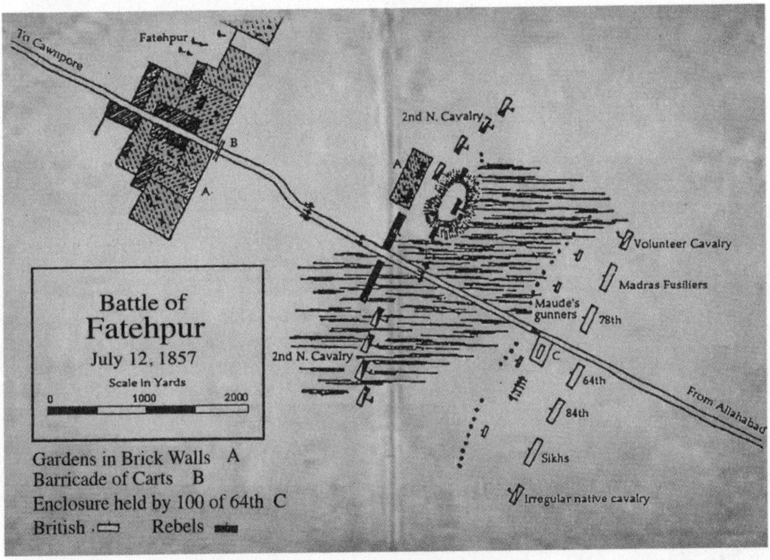

Map of Fatehpur. Author's collection.

'Knock over that chap on the elephant,' Havelock's Deputy-Adjutant General yelled to Captain Maude of the artillery, who subsequently fired a round shot up the elephant's vitals, sending none other than Tatya Tope tumbling to the ground, unhurt but chagrined.

Now the Highlanders moved forward down the road, chasing off the rebels who were trying to reclaim their damaged guns, and advanced in a wavering line that straddled the road and dipped down into the squelchy swamps. The Enfields' accuracy and rapidity of fire demonstrated why the Quartermaster General had been in such a hurry to introduce them to India. But a good many of them jammed, and the neophytes among the Fusiliers kept loading their cartridges backward and misreading their sights, sending their fire high over their enemies' heads. Nevertheless, with an effective range of 300 yards, enough found their targets to terrorize the sepoys. According to one of Havelock's men, the rebels' own lighter-charged musket balls fell among the British 'spent and harmless as autumn leaves'.

The British beat their way to the barricaded gates of Fatehpur and broke into the city, driving the rebels through the gardens and narrow streets. But a search for food and drink began to slow the Highlanders' progress, and 'the Sykeses', as the British soldiers called the Sikhs, halted to stuff their pouches with silver rupees from an overturned cart. This delay gave the retreating mutineers time to regroup on the far side of town, and for a moment it appeared that the rebel sowars, unopposed by Havelock's wavering Indian horsemen, might turn the General's right flank. But despite the surprising accuracy of the rebels' gunners and the 'astonishing rapidity' of their sowars, the sepoys could not hold their ground for long against Havelock's renewed assault and began to recede up the Grand Trunk Road.

At a cost of twelve men dead—all of them from sunstroke—by noon of 12 July Henry Havelock had won the first British victory since the uprising began.

There was ample plunder for everyone, for the Europeans' abandoned houses were full of 'ladies' dresses, men's overcoats, saddles, pictures, etc., from the sack of Kanpur', including Wheeler's own white saddle cloth, stored there by the rebels. Any sepoy Havelock captured was hanged 'without ceremony or delay'.

13 July
Havelock

A young Henry Havelock before the Persia campaign whitened his hair. Known as a courageous, pious, flinty Scot, he was beloved by the troops he relentlessly urged forward. He died after his attempt to relieve Lucknow. Author's collection.

The next morning, Havelock's Sikhs put Fatehpur to the torch. The rebels' defeat enraged Nana Sahib, who ordered another force sent out, this time under the command of his brother Bala Rao, with orders to 'kill all those men in the dirty shirts and blue caps'—the Enfield-toting Fusiliers—who 'kill all my men before they fire'.

The relief force subjected Fatehpur to some of their bitterest reprisals because an evangelical Collector who had been lionized by the New Lights was murdered here and his head displayed on a pike. Author's collection.

15 July
The Battle of Aong

Day and night, Havelock's column marched unopposed towards Kanpur. At dawn on 15 July, near the village of Aong, his scouts came upon a heavily fortified rebel position with two guns and a substantial body of mutineers preparing themselves for the column's arrival.

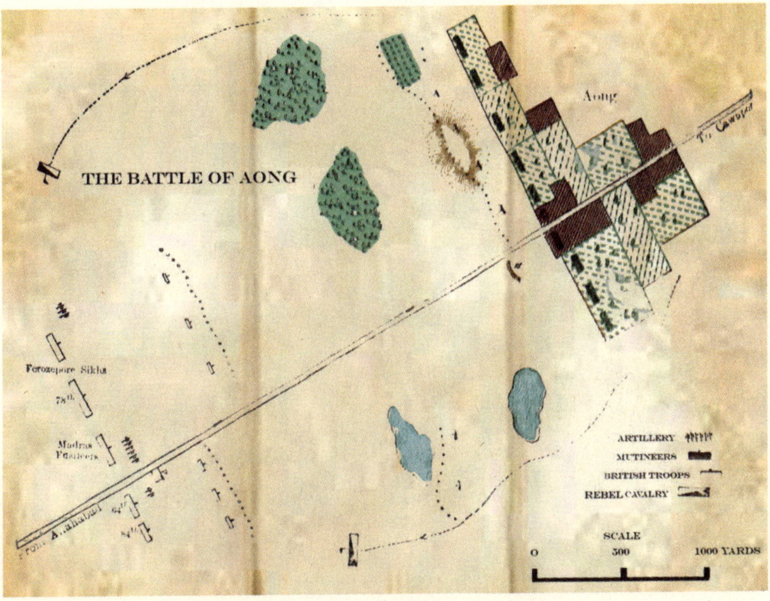

The Battle of Aong. Author's collection.

Havelock sent a third of his column ahead to meet the rebels, retaining the rest to guard the baggage train, which was threatened now by bold bands of rebel cavalry 'hovering on both flanks'. Major Renaud routed the sepoys from the village, but during the attack one rebel at least had the satisfaction of shooting this wholesale arsonist and hangman in the leg, driving a portion of his scabbard into the muscle of his thigh.

The 78th Highlanders taking the rebel guns at Aong.
Author's collection.

In the meantime, Maude's gunners fired so accurately at the mutineers' position on the road that a round shot not only killed a rebel gunner but 'jammed itself with the utmost neatness into the muzzle of the gun'. Back at Havelock's position the sowars tried to cut their way to the bullock train, but the British soldiers flung them back, and within a few minutes the rebels were fleeing the British Enfields once again, strewing the road with discarded weapons and plunder.

15 July
The Battle of Pandu Nadi

A few miles further on, the Grand Trunk Road crossed a broad stream called Pandu Nadi. Lacking boats and pontoons, Havelock would need the bridge to get his troops across, but only two hours after the

Battle of Aong, his spies reported that under the command of Nana's brother Bala Rao the rebels had fortified themselves just across the bridge and mined one of its three stone arches. Havelock ordered his men back to their feet and marched them two hours longer under the midday sun.

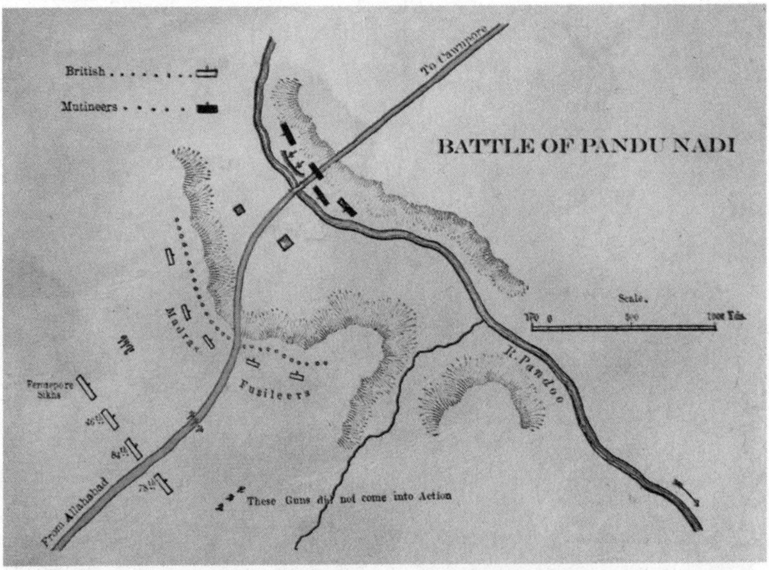

The Battle of Pandu Nadi. Author's collection.

Suddenly artillery opened up on them, and they fell back, lying flat on the ground as the old General squinted through his telescope down the simmering road. The near end of the bridge jutted out from a high bluff at the apex of the river's curve, where the road followed the middle of three parallel ravines. Across the bridge in the crook of the river the rebels were entrenched in great numbers on a gradual slope, equipped with 24- and 25-pounder guns.

Havelock sent his Fusiliers down the outer ravines, from where they spread out along the upper reaches of the riverbank and opened fire, managing to wound Bala Rao himself in the right shoulder. The rest of Havelock's infantrymen lay on the ground, covering their heads with their arms, as the rebel gunners fired in front of them while Maude's battery, arrayed in a vast arc and firing from only 600 yards, lobbed their round shot into the rebel position.

The first rebel round shot struck three soldiers in the legs, and as more cannonballs came skipping across the muddy ground, one young soldier lying near Havelock had just raised his head onto a pillow of earth when a round shot skimmed it from his shoulders.

The Battle before Kanpur. Author's collection.

There was a loud explosion, and the men peeked up from the ground to see that the rebels had detonated a mine, and a great cloud of dust and stone was rising from the bridge. When the smoke cleared, however, they saw that the mine had taken a mere bite out of the roadway. Havelock's gunners fired so accurately into Bala Rao's battery that they killed Bala Rao's elephant and broke the rebels' sponge staves, without whose cleansing application their muzzles would spark and explode. Now a detachment of Fusiliers came thundering across the cratered bridge with the Highlanders following behind, stabbing the stymied gunners with their bayonets, and chasing the rest into the river to drown.

As the sowars galloped away, Havelock hurried the rest of his troops across the bridge and halted a mile beyond.

15 July
The Bibighar

As Nana Sahib's bloodied army fell back into Kanpur, it was just as Azimullah had warned his liege all along: leave one feringhee alive, and he will multiply and destroy you. All Nana had accomplished with his mercies was to provoke the English into performing superhuman feats of courage and endurance to rescue the survivors. Had the British shown any such mercy to the people who lived along who lived along the Grand Trunk Road, the villagers whose homes and crops they burned, the furloughed sepoys and poor ryots they hanged, the women and children who had died by the hundreds in the flames and crossfire? Why should Nana extend his hospitality to the wives and children of such beasts?

HOUSE AT CAWNPORE, THE SCENE OF THE MASSACRE.

The Bibighar's central courtyard. Author's collection.

Nana may well have deemed himself thanklessly merciful. He had spared the prosperous Greenways and Jacobis, albeit for ransoms that never materialized. Never mind the massacre at Sati Chaura, he had spared not only the surviving women and children, but also the three Fatehgarh burra sahibs, albeit on the preposterous promise that they could persuade the British to withdraw from Allahabad in exchange for the lives of Nana's captives. But all of that had been for naught, and the British field force, though outnumbered, was relentless. It all came down to the old saw Azimullah had been citing since the uprising began: 'To extinguish the fire and leave the spark, to kill a snake and preserve its young, is not the wisdom of sensible men.'

The more faint-hearted among that dismal and disconsolate gathering may have harboured another motive, which was to eliminate all witnesses who might testify against them if in the end the British prevailed. If the problem was that the British were fighting with inhuman fury to save the women and children, then perhaps the solution was to cease their onslaught by leaving no women and children to rescue.

What Nana made of these arguments has never been determined. He may well have seen the logic of eliminating witnesses and would have felt betrayed by his prisoners, especially the Fatehghar burra sahibs. And it is possible that the decision to destroy them may have contributed to his new found resolution on the field of battle. But, months later, during their long flight from the British, Nana Sahib and Tatya Tope, even at their most defiant, would insist that they took no part in the decision to massacre the women and children.

With Havelock's column menacing the city, there was no time to dawdle over the matter when so many other seemingly more vital questions remained. How many men could the insurgency muster from its shrinking ranks at Kanpur? How many had fled? Were there enough lascars and bullocks to bring the artillery to the fork in the road? Who would protect Nana's household at Bithur? Where would they go if they were defeated? Where would they go if they won? To Delhi? Allahabad? Benares? The British had defeated all of his commanders. Now Nana Sahib himself must lead the troops. Who would join him in his stand at Aherwa?

Some 100 yards from Nur Mahomed's hotel, the begum reigned supreme at the Bibighar. She cut her staff of servants down to a female sweeper and a cook. When even the clothes Nana had provided became fouled with sweat, mud, and the offal from the sick and wounded, the women were obliged to do their own laundering.

In the thorns of the tree in the courtyard the women hung their laundry out to dry, crowding beneath the dripping cloth to seek shelter against the burning sun. Some probably attempted, with whatever black cloth they could find, to fashion widows' armbands to honour their dead husbands. A few still wore the bonnets and sun hats they had brought with them from the Entrenchment. Others covered their heads with wetted veils torn from the remnants of their gowns and petticoats. Most no longer had shoes to wear, and padded across the muck of the courtyard in their bare feet.

The deaths from disease continued. The Greenways, who with Mrs Jacobi and her children, were still sequestered from the other prisoners, suffered two losses in two days. First their ayah died on the thirteenth, and then Rose's grown son Edward the next day, both dehydrated by severe bouts of diarrhoea. So many women and children were ill by now that the Bengali doctor simply listed diarrhoea as the cause of death instead of trying to differentiate among cholera, dysentery and sepsis.

The begum had endeared herself to no one but her malicious lover, a Eurasian bodyguard named Sarvur Khan. The Bibighar's sepoy guards, especially their Jemadar Yusuf Khan, had grown to detest her queenly airs. Through the swarms of flies the begum paraded, officiously barking gratuitous commands at the servants and inmates, contemptuously averting her eyes from the children's wretchedness and covering her nose and mouth against the stench.

By the dawn of 15 July she presided over some 200 prisoners. Of these the three burra sahibs from Fatehgarh were the only grown men; 73 were women; and about 124 were children, including teenaged girls and boys. Early in the morning of the 15th, while lying on the filthy grass mats that covered the Bibighar's floors, the women could feel the earth shake and hear the muffled pounding of artillery somewhere south-east of the station. Shushing their children, they pressed their ears against the ground, listening for over an hour to the sporadic rumbling, like some distant echo of the Entrenchment barrages they had somehow survived. Outside the Bibighar, the guards were also listening, too discomposed to puff on their morning chillums.

Had the pounding approached or receded? The women asked themselves as the firing dwindled away. Had the rebels driven back the relief force that old Sir Hugh had promised for so long? Why ever had the firing stopped?

But then the roaring started up again, closer now and more intense, rolling across the station like a tide. Women seated by the Bibighar's windows could see that fewer guards were standing about, and those that remained were speaking excitedly, clustered in little groups and anxiously glancing back over their shoulder at the Bibighar and the Old Kanpur Hotel beyond.

Soon the rumbling was nearly drowned out by the rising clamour of panicked townspeople fleeing towards Bithur. As the gunfire dwindled again in the late hours of the morning, there was a burgeoning sense of expectancy in the humid noonday air, as if dark congested clouds were about to break.

In the stillness of the simmering afternoon, after the artillery fire from Pandu Nadi had died away, the surviving three male Fatehgarh fugitives must have known that whatever might befall the women and children in the Bibighar, they were doomed. At about four o'clock in the afternoon, Nana Sahib led his entourage up to the north-western perimeter of the Old Kanpur Hotel's compound and sat under a neem tree to await their execution.

First a few Indian spies were hustled out of a cell in the Bibighar's yard and brought before the Peshwa and beheaded. And then, as a crowd gathered, the burra sahibs were stood up against a wall and shot to death.

What exactly followed in the Bibighar when the Nana Sahib's guards received the order to execute the women and children can hardly be imagined, and has no place perhaps, in a battlefield guide, except to explain some measure of the rage of Havelock's relief force when they entered Kanpur two days later.

First a squad of sepoys was ordered to shoot the women and children from the windows. But they apparently fired into the ceiling and refused to reload. A second squad was assembled to replace the first and fired a volley into the panicked crowd, but a third line of sepoys, seeing what horrors the second had perpetrated, refused to fire.

Hussaini Khanum told them she would find real men for the job, and sent word to her lover, Sarvur Khan, to assemble his own execution squad. A little before sunset, Khan appeared, walking out of the setting sun in his red bodyguard's uniform and trailing four companions, each with a tulwar in his hand. As men and boys sat along the compound walls to watch, Khan and his cohorts stepped into the Bibighar and began methodically to slash at the survivors until, by nightfall, their bodies lay in a quivering heap. Sarvur Khan and his cohorts could do no more in the darkness and, locking the doors behind them, emerged into the courtyard with their arms and feet and clawed clothing covered in blood.[5]

16 July
The Battle of Aherwa

At four in the morning of 16 July, Havelock roused his exhausted troops to report that the Kanpur garrison had not been entirely wiped out after all, and that over 200 women and children were still held prisoners by the rebels.

'With God's help, men,' Havelock exhorted, 'we will save them, or every man of us die in the attempt.' The troops gave a cheer and began marching into the heat of what would prove to be the hottest day of the expedition, each man laden with sixty rounds of ball ammunition and whatever plunder they had retained. As the sun rose, a few toppled over from sunstroke, but their comrades could only drag them into the wayside shade for the baggage train to retrieve.

By noon they had gloomily tramped some sixteen miles, and, as they paused to rest, scouts returned with two deserters from Nana's army. In the dirt by Havelock's boots, they drew the fork in the Grand Trunk Road that lay three miles ahead: the left tine led to the city, and the right to the cantonments. By now, Teeka Singh had at last persuaded Nana Sahib to leave his suite in the Old Kanpur Hotel, mount his war elephant, and, to the beat of kettle drums, take command of his army. It was at this fork in the road, before the little village of Aherwa (present-day Ahirwan), that Nana Sahib awaited Havelock with 5,000 of his finest troops and eight heavy guns.

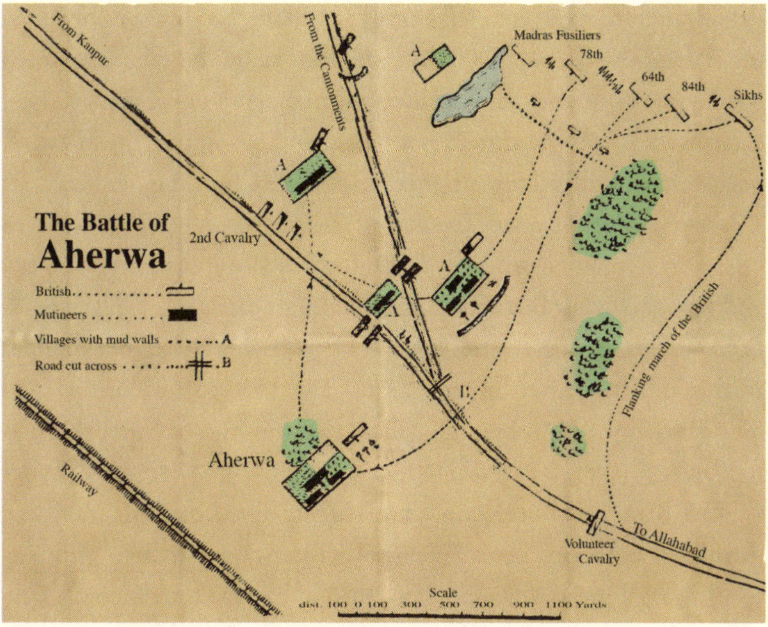

Map of the Battle of the Aherwa. Author's collection.

Havelock could see that to march directly into such a position would be suicide. His only chance was to attack the rebels' flank, and fortunately for him three groves of mango trees stood in a thousand-yard line in front of the rebel position. So, he ordered his volunteer cavalry to the front to act as decoys and trot directly towards the rebel centre, as if leading the foot soldiers on a frontal assault, while the bulk of his infantry turned abruptly to the right and crept behind the mango grove to attack the rebels' left flank.

By now Havelock's men had flooded their empty stomachs with 40 barrels of porter that the rebels had discarded, possibly on purpose, in a nearby swamp. Leaving the baggage behind, Havelock led them along the road for two miles. Now more men, reeling and dehydrated from alcohol, fell along the wayside, crying out for water, until the groves of mango trees came into view, and what remained of Havelock's infantry and artillery turned off the road and trudged silently across a flooded field as a rebel band, playing in the distance, performed an infuriating approximation of 'Cheer, boys, cheer'.

Havelock's dodge worked at first. There was no tell-tale dust to raise as the infantry proceeded 1,000 yards along the grove of trees, and the rebels kept bowling their round shot directly down the road. But through a gap in the trees one of Nana's gunners caught a glimpse of the soldiers' red coats and tartans and ordered his comrades to redirect their fire, sending their shot whistling and crashing through the trees.

The British did not return fire at first, but continued tramping through the flooded fields and among the swampy mango groves as rebel shot plunged around them, raising a great brown spray. The sepoys desperately wheeled about to meet the British, but were still scrambling into position when the column emerged from behind the third grove and advanced on the rebels' left.

Half of Nana's guns were now useless to him, for he could not fire without killing his own troops. Nevertheless, his three 24-pounders, positioned on high ground behind sturdy mud walls, raked the British ranks as they charged forward. Havelock's field guns were proving too light to reach their targets, and his infantry lay down now as the rebels' shot skipped across the fields.

Havelock's first horse had been shot out from under him. Now, bare-headed and erect on a hastily requisitioned nag, he rode up to the 78th and ordered them to their feet. To shrill Highland cries and the whine of bagpipes they quick-marched into the heat and the rebels' heavy fire, unleashing a murderous volley.

Abandoning their guns, the sepoys fell back in two waves, one massing 100 yards towards the cantonment, the other clustering behind a howitzer set in the centre of the branch road. Almost overcome with emotion, Havelock called on his Ross-shire Buffs once again. 'Now, Highlanders,' he cried, 'another charge like that wins the day!'

With the 64th running alongside, the 'petticoated devils', as the rebels called them, overran the howitzer, stabbing the gunners with their bayonets, as eighteen volunteer horsemen galloped into the midst of an advance party of sowars, bloodying their swords and helping to scatter the rebels up the cantonment road.

Havelock's men were exhausted and sinking in the terrible afternoon heat, and Nana was proving a more tenacious commander than his generals. In the waning evening light, Nana's gunners opened up an effective fire from two cannon set in the crook of the fork in the road.

Riding his nag among his recumbent troops, Havelock asked them, who would take the village: 'the Highlanders, or the 64th?' Running now on nothing but alcohol and adrenalin, men of both regiments rose to their feet once again and, charging forward with a cheer that was 'more like a howl', they took the rebel battery. But as if drawing on some inexhaustible supply of artillery, Nana somehow brought yet another heavy gun into play, and as his round shot whistled and bounded towards them, Havelock's exhausted and discouraged advance detachment could only lie flat on the ground.

Nana Sahib himself could be plainly seen riding to and fro with his entourage, reviving his troops' spirits with a din of trumpets, cymbals and drums. Heartened by the sight of the Highlanders lying upon the field, the rebels rallied and regrouped, and Nana's sowars jubilantly rode forward to envelopeo Havelock's prostrate troops as Maude's panicked artillery bullocks struggled in vain to draw their guns across the swampy ground.

By now perhaps 100 British soldiers had fainted from the heat, and Havelock could see that a few more minutes of prostration and paralysis could cost him the battle. So, there was nothing for it but once again to order his warriors to their feet, despite rebel fire of 'such precision and determination', wrote Havelock, 'as I have ever witnessed'.

As the Highlanders rose to their feet, the rebels' shot toppled them like bowling pins, spraying their hastily formed ranks with flesh and blood and strewing the field with the wounded. But, strangely provoked by the rebels' music, 'Havelock's Ironsides', as they came to be known, kept marching in lock step to within 300 yards of the guns and then, with Havelock's own son and aide-de-camp leading the way, charged forward into the smoke and grapeshot that kept belching from the cannon's muzzle.

'The mutineers fought fiercely and well,' wrote an officer. But as the British infantry closed in with their seventeen-inch bayonets, the rebels fired high and Maude's newly arrived guns poured round shot into Nana's ranks, until, amid ferocious hand-to-hand combat, the rebels fired one last volley and retreated towards Kanpur for good.

Searching Aherwa in the gloaming, the Highlanders came upon a pond entirely filled with the rebel dead, and in another hamlet, they finished off 300 wounded rebels. But Havelock's soldiers were utterly drained. 'Cartloads' of men had been laid low by 'sore feet and sunstrokes'; almost 100 more were wounded. With 'nothing but dirty ditch water to drink', many more were suffering from dysentery and cholera that seemed to rise like a poisonous miasma from the trampled mud of their encampments.

16 July
The Bibighar

By dawn, word of the previous night's massacre had spread throughout Kanpur and, despite the general exodus from the city, hundreds—some even said thousands—assembled at the Bibighar to view the carnage. Townsfolk, villagers, sepoys, gawking boys: they sat along the walls and crowded around the compound gates to see if what they had heard was true.

Around eight in the morning, the crowd parted to make way for a burial party of mehtars and four jullads led by a resourceful executioner named Aitwurya. By now they were expert at this sort of thing. But today's task was unusual in one respect: the bodies were to be dumped not into the Ganga this time but down an irrigation well some forty feet north of the Bibighar, and in some cases that would require dismemberment. A few prisoners had survived and had to be dispatched, including a boy who escaped from under his mother's skirts and ran in circles around the well.

Despite the squad's efforts, the remains completely engorged the throat of the Bibighar's well, and the rest of the corpses had to be piled into the back of a scavenger's cart. As the cart creaked off towards the river, Aitwurya and his jullads collected their sacks of gewgaws and heaps of bloody cloth and headed for their homes.

After his defeat at Aherwa that evening, Nana entirely circumvented the city. Drenched in sweat and mounted on a chestnut horse, he hurried his shattered army up to Bithur as Havelock's advance party approached the cantonment.

17 July
The Bibighar

The next morning, 17 July, Havelock assigned two doctors to accompany an advance detachment of the 84th into the cantonment to rescue and tend to the women and children he assumed remained alive. As they marched up the road in the dim light, a rumour rustled through their ranks that the rebels had massacred the women and children they had fought so furiously to rescue. But they were sick of rumours.

The road Havelock followed into Kanpur. National Army Museum.

Hugging the shadows of battered walls, they gazed at the charred and tumbled remains of European bungalows in compounds littered with 'broken furniture and crockery [and] leaves of books' and surrounded by scorched trees, their jagged branches stark against the hot morning haze. To their right they passed close by the ruins of St. John's Church, 'unroofed and dismantled', its memorial slabs and monuments destroyed. It appeared as though everything south of the Ganga Canal had been demolished: barracks, stables, bungalows, storehouses. The destruction had been total; even the doors, windows, shutters, gates had been ripped away and all the compound walls laid low.

Beyond the ruins of the telegraph office, they could see several buildings were still standing: the Old Kanpur Hotel, the Theatre, the Masonic Lodge, and the celebrated Assembly Rooms, where only months before the garrison had gathered for candlelit banquets and glittering balls. As they neared the Assembly Rooms, Wheeler's principal spy, the cattle gomashta (Company agent) Lalla Bhudri Nath, emerged from his hiding place and, out of the soldiers' earshot, conferred with the officers, pointing sorrowfully towards the river. As they proceeded into the compound of Sir George Parker's large charred bungalow, a trio of Indians—servants by the look of them—flitted anxiously around the gate, pointing towards the Bibighar and murmuring, 'Sahib! Sahib!'

The officers swung open the Bibighar's doors as a swarm of plump flies rose like swirling cinders from a bloody floor littered with ladies' bonnets and sun hats, children's shoes, papers, long tresses of ladies' hair. But where were the women and children? One after another the Highlanders crept towards the Bibighar and stood a moment at the threshold, gazing at the bloody desolation 'with wet eyes and quivering lips'. Pushed forward by their crowding comrades, a few staggered into the courtyard, where the bloody matting 'oozed spongily under their tread'. One officer declared that 'the scene he saw was the most awful that eye could witness'.

There is some controversy over what exactly the officers saw. This rendering appears to jibe with the first-hand accounts: a bloody handprint, gore everywhere amid a clutter of the victim's possessions, including a prayer book, ladies' sun hats hanging from the rafters and a number of broken water jugs, which may account for why, despite the heat, the sanguinary floor was still wet. National Army Museum.

In this image from the Illustrated Times, *the Bibighar has taken on palatial dimensions, dwarfing the soldiers and Indians, and including messages—'Countrymen avenge us', 'Countrymen think of us'—daubed in blood, which were in fact added by the soldiers General Neill marched through the building to inflame them.* Author's collection.

He was mistaken. For now, three Highlanders were following a bloody trail through the crushed grass and brush, forty feet from the Bibighar to the tangled roots of a clump of trees, where they found Bhudri Nath covering his mouth with his shawl and leaning over the lip of the Bibighar's well. The Highlanders joined him, and peered down into 'a mass of gory confusion'.

In this postcard image taken from the British Library's Mutiny Scroll, *two officers approach the mouth of the Bibighar well.* Author's collection.

Few whose sensibilities have been battered by the horrors of twentieth-century genocide and warfare can imagine how the sight of the women and children's hacked limbs and naked bodies enraged even Havelock's battle-hardened troops.

Britain's yellow press was quick to conjure rapacious mutineers with their torches and bloody tulwars bursting upon British motherhood. But, perhaps because of caste restrictions and soldierly pride, there were no credible reports that the rebels raped British women. Author's collection.

THE BRITISH LION'S VENGEANCE ON THE BENGAL TIGER.

The weakness of the symbolism in this propagandist cartoon from Punch *is that no lion is any match for a tiger.* Author's collection.

As soon as Havelock set off to relieve the Lucknow garrison, General Neill, left in command at Kanpur, issued what he called his 'strange law', condemning any man who took 'an active part in the mutiny' to enter the Bibighar and clean a portion of the blood on the floor in a manner 'as revolting to his feelings as possible', to be flogged if he resisted, and then to be hanged. 'All the Brahmins will be buried,' he decreed, 'and the Mohammedans burned.' He employed untouchables as executioners in order to condemn high-caste Hindus to an eternity of monstrous incarnations.[6]

Hanging parties added their own atrocious touches by forcing the condemned to ingest pork and beef and anything else that might violate their religion and break their caste. Many were beaten so badly that they were half dead by the time they reached the gallows, and in some cases their executioners would playfully fashion nooses so that the rope would break, thus condemning their captives to multiple drops.

Photographed before the uprising, a gloomy, sun-struck General James George Smith Neill already looks inclined to launch his atrocious campaign against any Indian even remotely suspected of supporting the insurgency. Author's collection.

Anyone found with European possessions was hanged, which meant that among the squads' victims were cantonment servants, many of whom had risked their lives to smuggle sustenance to their sahibs and memsahibs and protect their property. But British observers reported—some with respect but most with maddening disappointment—the vast majority met their fates with equanimity.

JUSTICE.

This uncharacteristically sombre Punch *cartoon expressed the indignation that swept Britain upon receiving news of the massacres at Kanpur.* Author's collection.

The earliest known photograph of the Bibighar shows two Indians posed for scale in front of the bank of the well before it was bricked over and the Bibighar and its enclosure demolished. Spectators watched the massacre and the burial seated along Bibighar's walls and the high wall that divided Sir George Parker's compound from a local road. Author's collection.

Soldiers roaming the Bibighar's environs found such keepsakes as a manicure set, a lock of hair clinging to a bramble, a child's shoe, and sent them home as mementoes. Left: Perhaps the most poignant keepsake is this marbles box that one of the Seppings children was still gripping when he was flung into the well on the morning of 16 July. Centre: Soldiers kept swatches of cloth they found around the well. This one bears a caption: 'This piece of silk was found near the Well at Cawnpore (immediately after that place was recaptured) by an officer of the 93rd Highlanders and supposed to have belonged to one of

the unfortunate ladies who were massacred there and thrown down the well.' Right: Some soldiers whittled pieces of the Bibighar's mulsuri tree into crosses and coffins. This is one of twenty carved by officers of HM 32nd to honour their dead. Courtesy of Mark Probett.

A British gallows. From left to right: Two of six police with tulwars stand upon ground littered with hangmen's rope, as a turbaned British officer looks on, standing over one of the two stanchions that have been kicked out from under the two accused rebels. To the right, the squad's next victim, hands and ankles bound, awaits his fate standing between his low-caste escorts. Author's collection.

31 July–13 August
Havelock

This is not the place to recount Havelock's campaign to relieve the besieged garrison at Lucknow, except to say that when he and his ailing troops were twice forced to fall back to the river, General Neill took it upon himself to accuse his superior of shirking. But then Neill received word that Tatya Tope, Nana Sahib's most gifted tactician, was marching on Kanpur ahead of the mutinous Gwalior Contingent, a professional army that the British had trained to keep watch over the Marathas. Now, suddenly, Neill began imploring Havelock to return with his men to defend the station.

On 13 August, Havelock led his cholera-ridden troops back across the Bridge of Boats, humiliated, restive and fed up with Neill's vaunting insubordination. By now Kanpur's dust and clay had turned to mud, and never suspecting that this was the chief cause of cholera, his men cooled themselves by splashing about in the monsoon lake that had been Kanpur's parade ground.

16 August
The Battle of Bithur

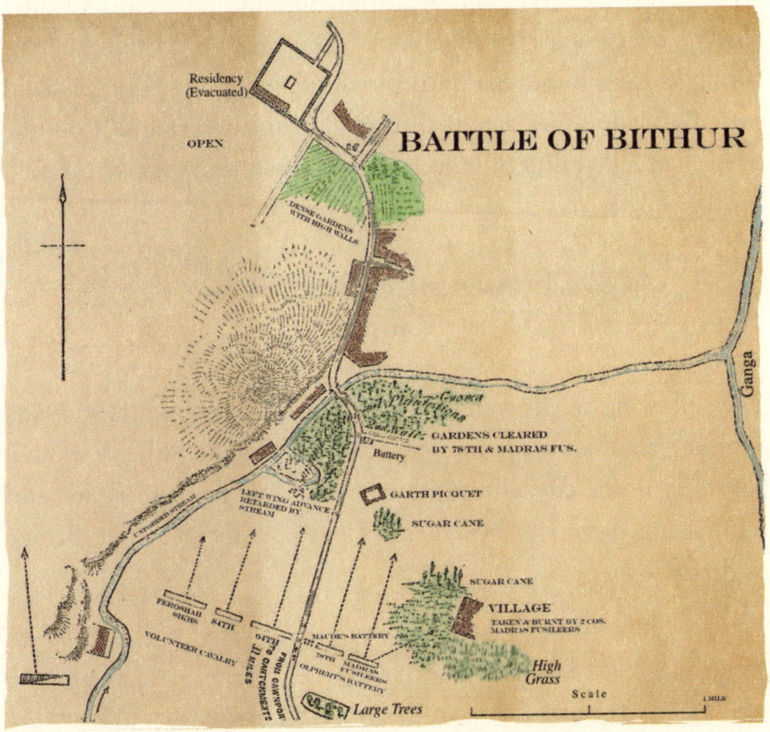

Map of the Battle of Bithur. Author's collection.

Intelligence had reached Havelock that a rebel force was massing in Bithur, intending eventually to join Tatya Tope's assault on Kanpur. With two heavy guns, and five sepoy and two sowar regiments at their disposal, they apparently did not fear an attack from Havelock's ailing and depleted force.

After his twin retreats to the river, however, and his flight across the Bridge of Boats, Havelock was determined to redeem himself. On 16 August, he led his men to Bithur, where they were confronted by thousands of mutineers and matchlock-men positioned behind high mud walls and hidden among stands of corn and sugar cane.

The rebels were not only creditably deployed, but after Havelock unleashed a largely ineffectual cannonade, they fought his forces with bravery and determination: born, perhaps, of their outrage over Neill's 'strange law'. They gave no ground at first, falling in their hundreds until they were grappling hand to hand with the Madras Fusiliers. Before finally retreating from Bithur, the rebels had killed fifty of Havelock's men, while sunstroke claimed another dozen.

17 August–21 September
Kanpur

The following weeks were spent chasing down rumours of Nana Sahib's machinations, trying to establish some semblance of civil authority in the city, all the while terrorizing the countryside and reinforcing their 100-by-200-yard entrenchment by the Bridge of Boats.

British troops rampaging through Kanpur District. Author's collection.

On 3 September, the same James Outram who had exiled the Nawab of Awadh arrived at Kanpur. As the newly appointed Commander of the Kanpur Division, Outram outranked Havelock. But he made a show of bowing to his authority in another push to relieve Lucknow. With 3,000 men at their disposal, the newly organized and reinforced relief expedition marched into Awadh on 19 September and beat their way to the Lucknow Residency, only to end up so depleted that they were entrapped with the Lucknow garrison they had fought to free.

One happy result, as far as the leaders of the uprising were concerned, was that as Havelock's men battled their way through the streets, someone managed to fire a bullet through General James Neill's brain.

It is hard to imagine who would have been devastated by the death of General Neill: author of the 'strange law', self-appointed executioner, unpopular with all but his most sanguinary troops, and Havelock's insubordinate nemesis. Author's collection.

9 November
Kanpur

Sir Colin Campbell, KCB, as depicted on the cover of the sheet music for 'The Oriental March of Victory', composed in his honour by Stephen Glover. Author's collection.

The next worthy to turn up in Kanpur was Commander-in-Chief Sir Colin Campbell, a veteran of the Napoleonic Wars who, upon his arrival on 3 November, abolished General Neill's 'strange law' as 'unworthy of the English name and a Christian government'. He was determined to relieve Lucknow as soon as possible, then bring his might to bear on Tatya Tope and the Gwalior Contingent. On 9 November he crossed the Bridge of Boats, leaving Major General Charles Ash Windham and 500 men to defend Kanpur and express orders to never venture beyond their fortified position unless in its defence.

Windham was one of the few senior officers not to have disgraced himself in the Crimean War; he should have quit while he was ahead.
National Army Museum.

Though Windham was a bona fide hero of the Crimean War, he was also something of a windbag, which may explain why a man left in isolation with ambiguous orders and too few men to carry them out would be blamed for what followed. Though Campbell had initially instructed Windham to relay all troops arriving from other stations to join him in the relief of Lucknow, Windham persuaded

Campbell to allow him to retain some 1,200 troops as they arrived, in addition to the 500 men Campbell had left with him. As word reached him of Tatya's rapidly advancing force, Windham decided (against Campbell's orders) to deploy 1,400 bayonets in the field, with a cordon of Madras NI posted in a wide cordon to convince Tatya Tope that Windham commanded a formidable force.

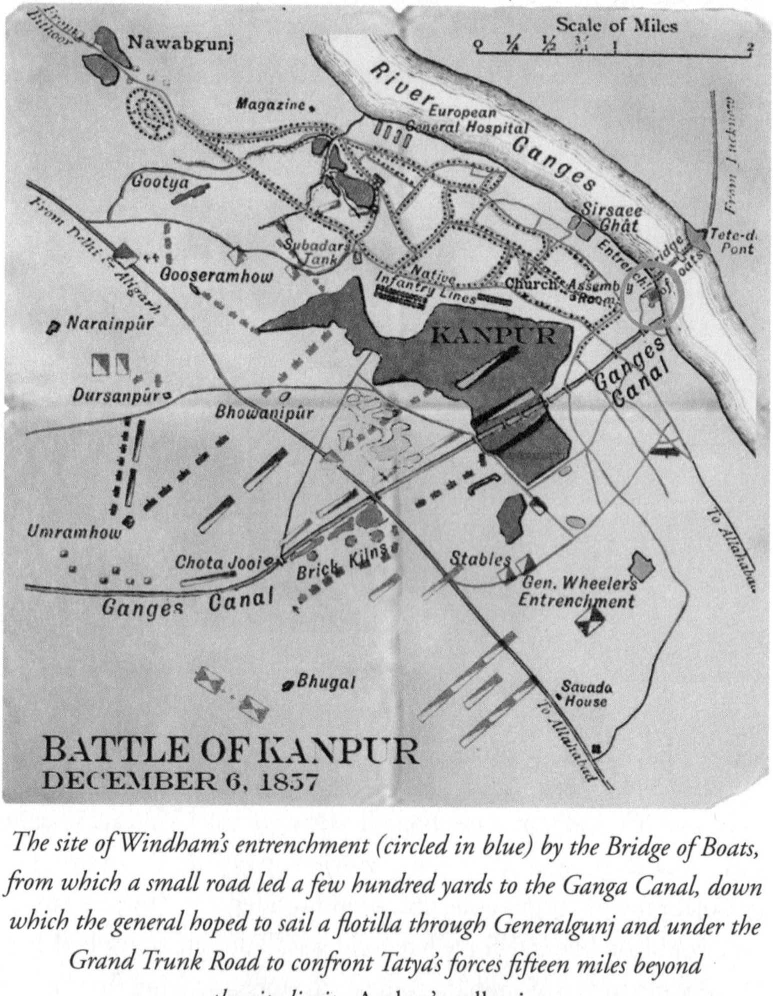

The site of Windham's entrenchment (circled in blue) by the Bridge of Boats, from which a small road led a few hundred yards to the Ganga Canal, down which the general hoped to sail a flotilla through Generalgunj and under the Grand Trunk Road to confront Tatya's forces fifteen miles beyond the city limits. Author's collection.

But Tatya Tope knew better. Closely tracking Campbell and Windham both, his spies provided him with a fairly accurate account of the relief force's movements and the Kanpur garrison's size. The most gifted commander of all the rebels, Tope was a short, burly and decisive man with a commanding gaze that burned under the thick grey hedgerow of his brow. After crossing the Yamuna river with thousands of troops, he had secured every principal town along his way.

Windham sought Campbell's approval of his advance up the Canal, but none came. On 19 November, he received a cryptic note from Campbell announcing that he had taken the Lucknow Residency and ordering Windham to await further instructions. But Windham didn't know what to make of this, as Havelock, who had since died of cholera, had 'taken' the Residency as well, only to be entrapped and besieged. In any case, no 'further instructions' were forthcoming: indeed, all communication with Lucknow had broken down.

As word reached him that Tatya Tope was joining forces with rebels from Awadh and advancing rapidly, Windham abandoned his plan to send his men down the Ganga Canal. Instead, he deployed most of his force in a complex of brick kilns on the city's outskirts.

By 25 November, Tatya Tope was ready to make his move. So, it appears, was Windham, who sent his men on an expedition to attack the rebels at the Pandu Nadi. His men proceeded with great confidence until they encountered a rebel battery firing grape. Battling through standing crops of sugar cane and corn, his men encountered 3,000 of Tatya Tope's Gwalior Contingent. The rebels fought with courage, skill and determination, and though they eventually fell back, it was not before killing sixteen of Windham's men and wounding seventy-eight.

Windham halted his troops to celebrate their victory, only to receive reports that the Contingent's main body was advancing on

Kanpur in good order and great numbers, and from several directions. The general ordered his advance party to withdraw five miles back to the brick kilns, thus confirming Tatya Tope's estimation of his strength. The next morning, while encamped on open ground, Windham's men awoke to the happy news that Tatya Tope had not yet crossed the Ganga Canal. But at 10 a.m. Tatya's artillery opened up, sending cannonballs plunging into Windham's tents.

By this time the general had divided his field force into two equal parts, with about 600 men occupying the kilns under a Brigadier Wilson, and the remainder somewhat forward of them. This second position, commanded by a Major Walpole, bore the brunt of what followed, but when Windham tried to reinforce Walpole, Tatya Tope cannily set his cavalry on them, and temporarily immobilized them with artillery, of which it was said he commanded fifty pieces. In the meantime, rebel forces the British no doubt overestimated at 25,000 men had taken the city, and were menacing the entrenchment itself. Hundreds of panicked local people piled into the works. Despite their officers' threats and whips, Windham's men abandoned their positions and raggedly fled to the entrenchment, where an elderly Sikh greeted them at the gate, shaking his head and declaring that Windham's men 'were not the brothers' of the men who had defeated the Sikh confederacy.

Now Thomson, Delafosse and Shepherd found themselves back where the nightmare began: in an entrenchment besieged by an overwhelming rebel force. Windham's fortification and the size of his command, complemented now by more arrivals from Allahabad, was far superior to Wheeler's. But then in numbers, artillery and discipline, Tatya Tope's command was far superior to Nana Sahib's.

Not every soldier had made his way to safety. Among those killed was Brigadier Wilson, who had tried to hold his position at the kilns. And it was reported that two stragglers from the 64th had been captured and summarily hanged from the gallows at the Bibighar. The Marathas and Awadhis wrought special horrors on the families of Campbell's Sikhs, murdering them and looting their temple.

Nana Sahib had meanwhile returned to Bithur, and the rest of his officers had joined forces with Tatya Tope. But beyond commanding vegetable sellers to keep their stalls open, the rebels did not attempt to govern the city they had occupied, for by now all of Kanpur lay in ruins, much of it razed and all of it raked by fire from both sides.

On 27 November, Campbell and an advance force arrived at the Bridge of Boats from his costly but successful rescue mission in Lucknow and began to send his convoy of 3,000 troops, 2,000 wounded men and non-combatants, artillery and spoils across the Ganga. A day later he entered the entrenchment, and was so appalled by the debacle at the brick kilns and Windham's retreat that he was for a time deaf to Windham's entreaties to commence an attack on Tatya Tope. Indeed, he spent so long conveying his command across the river and settling everyone into the entrenchment that he earned the nickname 'Sir Crawling Campbell'.

On the morning of the 29th, Tatya Tope's artillery launched a barrage so fierce as to 'intercept sight'. Thomson was proud that the battlements he had helped to design withstood the cannonade, but he was alarmed that once again the garrison would be encumbered by women and children.

They did not stay long. Campbell was determined not to mount a counterattack until after 3 December, when he could safely set the women and children he had rescued on the road to Allahabad.

By now he had added 5,600 reinforcements to his ranks and thirty-five heavy guns to his arsenal. With a force numbering almost 10,000 men, two days later he ordered a feint to the right with a thundering artillery barrage. Tatya Tope apparently fell for Campbell's ruse and ordered his men to meet it, and when Campbell unleashed the bulk of his men on a flanking attack on the left, the confusion and the fire from Campbell's heavy guns sent the Gwalior Contingent and its allies reeling.

It is hard to tell, but from Campbell's presence this illustration appears to depict his men driving the rebels out of the city. Author's collection.

Bitterly, the rebels set fire to what few buildings remained, with the exception of the theatre and the Assembly Rooms, which the British had employed as a storehouse and hotly defended. Soon they had abandoned the Ganga Canal and fled towards Kalpi with Campbell's cavalry in hot pursuit. Jettisoning their weapons and spreading out across the fields of corn and scrub, they proved easy prey for Campbell's plundering lancers. Nor did Campbell's men spare the rebel wounded they came upon lying in makeshift hospitals.

By nightfall on 6 December, what was left of Tatya Tope's army had withdrawn to Bithur, while in Kanpur it was as if the British had resurrected the late General Neill, for every local man even remotely suspected of aiding Tatya Tope was executed.

By the time Campbell sent a column into Bithur, Nana Sahib had fled by boat across the Ganga, and the few loyal rebels who remained behind to cover his escape were quickly dispatched. What followed was the energetic looting of Nana Sahib's palace. British sappers were promised a share in any plunder they found, and eventually they focused their efforts on a well on the palace grounds which they dredged in rotating shifts, pulling out of the muck Nana Sahib's tarnished silver ceremonial howdah and no end of golden plates and gewgaws. They pried semi precious stones out of Nana Sahib's temple and blew it to atoms; the only residence they did not entirely destroy was that of the Sikh whose family had contributed six acres to Baji Rao II and who had chastised Windham's panic-stricken men when they retreated into the Entrenchment. Its ruins stand on a promontory and are often mistaken for the remains of Nana Sahib's palace.

In 1982, 125 years after the uprising, many structures the British razed along Bithur's waterfront still lay in ruins. Photograph by Andrew Ward.

Epilogue

Kanpur. Though Kanpur soon returned to its former role as a staging area for the campaigns against the rebels, with Tatya Tope's defeat and the pillaging of Bithur, the Kanpur uprising never extended beyond 1857. As the rebels were routed elsewhere, the city began to rebuild, and within twenty years, thanks in large part to the completion of the railway, it had become not only a garrison but an industrial hub, with factory chimneys replacing cannon barrels belching smoke.

Nana Sahib escaped into the malarial foothills of the Himalayas. He reportedly died soon afterward of malaria, but for the next fifty years reports came in that he was posing as a sadhu and trying to reignite a Maratha rebellion. So many spurious reports circulated, that when a young civil servant reported to his superiors that he had at last captured the 'Butcher of Bithur', he received a telegram commanding him to release him at once.

Nana Sahib suspect.
National Army Museum.

Azimullah Khan was last sighted heading towards Calcutta, suffering from smallpox. But he too disappeared. The rumour was that he eventually made his way to Istanbul as an emissary of the Sherif of Mecca. In any case, his small son ended up in the care of a Kanpur missionary who converted him to Christianity.

Tatya Tope capture, 1859.
Author's collection.

Tatya Tope took part in many subsequent engagements and led the British a merry chase until his capture in 1859. In this children's book illustration, Tatya Tope's betrayer skulks in the background as the warrior himself surrenders his tulwar to a British officer. Though Tatya Tope had proved a worthy foe at the Battle of Kanpur and in subsequent engagements, he was never forgiven for his alleged role in the attack at Sati Chaura. Before he was summarily executed, he was forced to pose for a watercolour sketch, after which an officer cut off one of his braids as a keepsake.

Hussaini Khanum, who had imperiously overseen the women and children at the Bibighar, managed to escape to the hills with Nana Sahib's entourage and was never seen again.

A number of captured rebels were tied to the muzzles of guns and blown into oblivion. But the business was ghastly as well as costly; the vast majority of executions were conducted by hanging parties, firing squads, and the random acts of individual soldiers. National Army Museum.

The mutineers. No one knows how many tens of thousands of mutineers were killed in battle, hunted down, captured, hanged—or, most famously, blown from guns. But after the first frenzy died down, local magistrates sentenced captive Indian troops to Port Blair, one of the Andaman Islands. It was a miserable, pestilential place whose agues killed off most of the first shipload. When 228 rebels tried to escape, disease and attacks by local aborigines killed twenty of them, and after the remainder turned themselves back in, the prison superintendent hanged eighty-one. But when the Viceroy, Lord Mayo, visited the colony in 1872, one convict sepoy at least had the great satisfaction of stabbing him to death.

Sepoy prisoners from the 1857 uprising built this vast penitentiary in the Andaman Islands, where twentieth-century independence workers would also be incarcerated. Fconaway at Wikimedia.

After the uprising, the British switched from recruiting Awadhis and high-caste Hindus to members of what they called the 'martial races': Sikhs, Gurkhas, Baluchis, Pathans.

Amy Horne Cook. The Cook children perished with their mother and father at Sati Chaura, but Amy survived as a sowar's concubine. After her rescue, she testified against her abductor and wrote a memoir of the experience. She eventually married and supported herself giving piano lessons in Calcutta.

Amy Horne. Author's collection.

Margaret Wheeler. Like Amy Horne, Margaret Wheeler was abducted by a sowar. The yellow press promulgated a story that rather than submit to his lust, she defiantly gunned down her abductor and his family and tossed herself into a well. But she embarrassed imperial propagandists by remaining with him the rest of her life. Apparently the sowar treated her more respectfully than she anticipated the British ever would have. As a very old lady she used to visit a British woman of a Sunday to drink tea, converse in English, and don Western clothing.

'The Death of Miss Wheeler'. Barely visible in the background, a sepoy is depicted hacking a baby to death. Author's collection.

William Jonah Shepherd helped relatives of the victims determine where and when they had died. He went on to write the definitive first-hand account of the uprising in Kanpur. He was rewarded by government with a jagir or rural estate, but he was too enfeebled by grief, guilt and shock to make a success of it. He died in poverty in 1891.

Jwala Pershad was captured in late 1859, and after testifying that in the foothills he had witnessed Nana Sahib's cremation, he was hanged at Sati Chaura, where, on 27 June, two years before, he had helped direct the attack on Wheeler's garrison.

Jwala Pershad just before his hanging. Collection of Mark Probett.

The boatmen. According to their descendants, the British flogged and executed the heads of the boatmen's guild for their role in the massacre at Sati Chaura and razed their village.

Nunne Nawab had commanded one of the more effective batteries during the siege, and remained so revered by Kanpur's Moslems that the British merely banished him to Mecca, where people sometimes confused him with Nana Sahib.

The Mehtars. A number of the low-caste men the British hired to restore order in Kanpur turned out to be some of the murderers of the women and children. One of these was Gungu Mehtar, who was hanged in 1858.[7]

Gungu Mehtar. Collection of Mark Probett.

Mowbray Thomson published his account of Kanpur to great acclaim in 1859, and became enough of a celebrity that he handed out autographed *cartes des visite* of himself to his admirers. After recuperating back in Britain, he was appointed political agent in Manipur and the Viceroy's agent overseeing King Wajid Ali Shah's exiled court. Though he retired in 1887 as a Major General, he was made a full General in 1896. He died in 1917.

Mowbray Thomson. Collection of Mark Probett.

The **Nawab of Farrukhabad** surrendered to an officer on a promise that his life would be spared. Though a court sentenced him to death for siding with the rebels and overseeing the massacre of his Fatehgarh captives, the officer's promise carried the day. He was eventually exiled to Aden at the mouth of the Red Sea. He apparently died in Mecca a few years later.

Nawab of Farrukhabad.
Collection of Zoë Yalland.

The Sati Chaura Memorial. One of the few Hindu temples in Kanpur that the British did not destroy was the Hardeo Temple, the scene of the attack on the boats. Unlike the Entrenchment and the Bibighar, it was hardly memorialized at all except for a gated cross bearing the legend 'In Memoriam/27 June/1857' that has long since disappeared. Perhaps as a result, Sati Chaura remains much as it was in 1857.

A 1920s postcard of the Hardeo Temple. Jwala Pershad and Gungu Mehtar were said to have been hanged from this tree. Author's collection.

A modern-day boatman rows up to the Hardeo Temple. On either side of the original temple residences have been built, one for the local pandit, to whom donations are encouraged. Photograph by Andrew Ward.

The Bibighar Memorial. Lord Canning left it to his wife and her sister Louisa, Countess of Waterford, to design a suitable monument. Louisa provided a sketch, which Lady Canning brought to engineer Henry Yule, and construction and landscaping began under the supervision of G.E. Lance and C.B. Thornhill, the brother of the Fatehgarh magistrate who had been killed outside the Bibighar.

The Bibighar well in 1858. Collection of Mark Probett.

The Celtic cross, erected by soldiers passing through Kanpur in November 1857, was the first memorial at the Bibighar well. Badly weathered and damaged, it reads, 'I believe in the resurrection of the body. I believe in the life everlasting'. Photograph by Andrew Ward.

Louisa's sketch for the Memorial Well. Courtesy of the Victoria and Albert Museum (permission pending).

For a sculptor, they chose Baron Carlo Marochetti, the husband of one of their childhood friends, who had designed the Cutari monument to commemorate the Crimean War. Louisa instructed the Baron to stick close to her rendering of a grieving angel. However, it was decided that her head should be more upright.

The Memorial Well became an icon, a reminder to subsequent generations of the terrible price their ancestors paid in the service of John Company. In British albums and postcards, it became an even more prominent subject than the Taj Mahal, and attracted thousands of visitors every year.

The Memorial Well set amidst a vast park dedicated to the Europeans who died in the uprising. Though no Indians, excluding malis [gardeners] were allowed to enter, they were obliged to contribute to a fund to cover its upkeep. Author's collection.

Fed up with British sanctimony, not long after India gained its independence in 1947, a crowd rushed into the park and set about demolishing the Memorial Well, but they were stopped before they could finish the job.

A piece of the Memorial Well's Gothic screen lying in Nana Rao Park.
Photograph by Andrew Ward.

Soon afterwards, Prime Minister Nehru magnanimously allowed British residents to move what remained of the monument, along with various other gravestones and memorials, to the grounds of All Souls, where they still stand, hard by the site of Wheeler's Entrenchment.

The remnants of the Memorial Well and Gothic screen as they stand today on the grounds of All Souls Church. Originally the screen completely surrounded Marochetti's angel and stood in the centre of what is now Nana Rao Park.
Photograph by Andrew Ward.

Exiled, her sheaves and wings repaired with mortar and wire, Marochetti's angel continues to keep her lonely vigil.
Photograph by Andrew Ward.

The Entrenchment

About half of the site of Wheeler's Entrenchment has been preserved on the grounds of All Souls Church on Memorial Lane. On a visit in 1876, Prince Edward had it demarcated with brick posts, most of which have since been pilfered. But even with the surrounding trees that have grown up long since, you can still get some idea of the sheer bleakness of the place.
Photograph by Andrew Ward.

But the penultimate memorial to Wheeler's doomed garrison is All Souls Church itself, a vast Lombardo Gothic pile that was erected in the 1870s over the redan in the north-east corner of the Entrenchment itself.

All Souls, redubbed Memorial Church by the Church of India.
Photograph by Andrew Ward.

The apse at All Souls is lined with marble plaques listing the names of all the Christians known to have died at Kanpur between 5 May and 16 July 1857.
Photograph by Andrew Ward.

Along its clerestory are stained glass windows memorializing the senior officers who perished at Kanpur, and brass plaques memorializing such protagonists as Thomson and Delafosse gleam from its columns.

A clerestory stained glass window bearing General Wheeler's name.
Photograph by Andrew Ward

On All Soul's grounds can be found many gravestones and regimental memorials. Some graves were reinterred on All Soul's grounds, but other stones stand where they were first erected. For instance, the gravestone marking the resting place of the earliest victims of the siege lies where the soldier's garden stood, just behind the long-demolished tile-roofed barrack.

This stone 'covers the remains, and is sacred to the memory of, those who were the first to meet their deaths, when beleaguered by mutineers and rebels in June 1857'. Among these was Lydia Hillersdon, wife of the collector, who was buried in a garden plot behind the tile-roofed barracks.
Photograph by Andrew Ward.

Draw a line between this gravestone and the Entrenchment well and you can orient yourself to the Entrenchment's layout.

The only surviving structure on the site of the Entrenchment is the well that served as the garrison's only source of water. Even at night, fetching bucketfuls was a perilous business because rebel snipers would hear the creak of its rope and open fire. Photograph by Andrew Ward.

Memorials to the Uprising. Most of the British memorials to the uprising are in the tradition-venerating Kanpur military cantonment, whose streets still retain the names of British generals. But Kanpur has not been favoured with many monuments to the leaders of the rebellion. What was once Memorial Park is now Nana Rao Park, the well and British gravestones have been removed, here and there are shards from the memorial screen, and from time to time the surrounding iron fence is painted in pastels. But there is little to remind the visitor of the park's history.

In Nana Rao Park, portions of the angel's pedestal were assembled into a Hindu shrine under a banyan tree known as the Boodhha Bargard (Old Banyan), from which it is said Neill hanged hundreds of suspected rebels. Local authorities were sharply criticized recently for cutting it down. (The sign advertised a local college.) Photograph by Andrew Ward.

A monument to Tatya Tope now occupies a corner of the Memorial Park, which was renamed Nana Rao Park around the time the bust was installed. There is some controversy about the location of the Bibighar well; the author believes that it is under the vast sandstone circle that has since been dedicated to the memory of Tatya Tope, upon which local children play cricket. Photograph by Andrew Ward.

Nana Sahib is memorialized with a bust in Bithur that was installed long after Independence. Photograph by Andrew Ward.

In Bithur, this ruin is sometimes mistaken for the remains of Nana Sahib's palace. But the British demolished that vast Maratha pile with dynamite and artillery until virtually nothing was left. This ruin is actually all that is left of the mansion of a local sardar: the same Sikh who donated six acres to accommodate Baji Rao II's exile and whose descendant, during Tatya Tope's attack on Windham's entrenchment, castigated British soldiers for retreating. Photograph by Andrew Ward.

Conclusion

THE KANPUR THEATRE OF THE uprising of 1857 included six major battles marked by great courage on both sides. But it is subsumed by the massacres it continues to evoke in the public imagination. Not since their calamitous flight from Kabul fifteen years earlier had the British suffered such a catastrophe as befell north India in 1857.

From first to last, rebel forces at Kanpur vastly outnumbered their British foes, and on the face of it they might have carried the day without resorting to subterfuge. But for all their numbers, they operated under some of the same disadvantages that plague mutinies everywhere.

One fundamental weakness was that they had discarded the officers who had trained and commanded them, and in some regiments killed their senior Indian officers as well. This amounted to a kind of regimental beheading that left many of them leaderless. Nana Sahib's titular leadership was feeble and vacillating, and his court's commands to fire on the embarking garrison and to massacre women and children had a corrosive effect on the mutineers' morale.

Even a skilled artillerist like Nunne Nawab and warrior like Tatya Tope could not overcome the mutineers' disunity. From the start, they were divided by regimental rivalry, class, rank, caste, religion, allegiance, language and regional origin. Only Tatya Tope and the Gwalior Contingent could lend cohesion to the struggle in and around Kanpur, but even they could not breach Windham's entrenchment nor sever the Bridge of Boats.

The insurgency did not win the unwavering support of Kanpur's moneyed interests who had profited from doing business with the British East India Company. Many of the moneylenders and cattle brokers denied the rebels their resources, and some even spied for the Company, providing vital information that the British could convey by telegraph all the way to Calcutta, while the rebels had to rely on couriers and relays. And what initial support the mutineers had gained from the ryots and taluqdars was soon neutralized by Neill's reign of terror.

Not to deprecate Havelock's accomplishment nor the astonishing defence of Wheeler's Entrenchment, but there were other factors that weighed against the insurgents. By rejecting the 1853 Enfields with their tainted cartridges, the mutineers were denied the use of a vastly superior weapon that was powerful enough and accurate enough to drop a man from a great distance. To repeat: 'Kill all those men in the dirty shirts and blue caps,' Nana Sahib had raged, referring to the Enfield-toting Madras Fusiliers. 'They kill all my men before they fire.'

What hampered the Kanpur insurgency was a combination of inferior weapons, outmoded tactics, poor communication, disenchantment with their vacillating commanders, divisions within their ranks and soldierly shame over the massacre of innocents, all in the doubtful and somewhat abstract cause of a return to feudalism. Though many fought to retaliate against British reprisals, they could not match the cohesion of the British crusade to defend, rescue and avenge their women and children.

The well at the Bibighar would bedevil subsequent efforts to rid India of British rule until 13 April 1919. On that day in Amritsar, tens of thousands of Punjabis ignored bans on assemblies to gather in Jallianwalla Bagh to celebrate a Sikh festival and protest the deportation of two independence workers. Without warning, Acting

Brigadier General Reginald Dyer turned up, blocked the main exits, and ordered his Gurkha Rifles to open fire. After they had fired over 1,600 rounds of ammunition into the crowd, at least a thousand lay wounded, hundreds more injured by the crush of the panicked crowd, and 400 men, women and children killed, 120 of them after jumping into a well. The Martyrs Well at Jallianwalla Bagh appalled and radicalized even moderate Indians who had hitherto trusted in the British Raj.

Up until World War II, the descendants of the fallen who visited Kanpur purchased elaborate tapestries of the Memorial Well that still turn up at flea markets all across the British Commonwealth.

Collection of Mark Probett.

Practical Information for Visitors

Kanpur may be best visited on a day trip from Lucknow, whose Residency ruins evoke so much of the insurgency of 1857, and which has retained at least a whiff of its nawabi elegance. Kanpur was always a drudge to its sister city across the Ganga, and remains an industrial hub: bustling, vital, prosperous, but also noisy, clogged and polluted. However, the relatively unscathed military cantonment itself remains much as it was during the Raj, all the way down to streets that retain their original names.

Getting there. There are numerous flights to Kanpur from Delhi, Agra and Allahabad, and express trains to Kanpur's recently refurbished Kanpur Central Station.

Hotels. There are two fairly well-regarded hotels in the cantonment, not far from Kanpur's primary historical sites. (*Note: When calling from outside India, dial 00 before the numbers given here.*) **The Status Club Resort** (tel. 91 51223 80706) at 58 Cantonment Road is only 1.7 km from Sati Chaura Ghat. The less expensive **Kingston Resort** (tel. 91 98397 64955) is on the Mall at 84 Cantonment Road and boasts a swimming pool. Within the old Civil Lines is the high-rise **Landmark Hotel** (tel. 91 84007 06868) on Somdat Plaza. *(Note: If you intend to make Lucknow your base of operations, historian Rosie Llewellyn-Jones recommends 'the long-established Taj Mahal Lucknow and the newer Lebua Lucknow Hotel set in a delightful 1930s traditional bungalow'; also, Clarks Awadh, 'an old, established well-situated hotel'.*

Transportation. Cycle rickshaws that accommodate two passengers are cheap and can circumvent bad traffic, but they also expose you to noise and pollution. There are a couple of fairly reliable car services in the city: **Car Cooper** (tel. 91 85889 49236) and **Kanpur Cab Services** (tel. 91 95654 9082), but the hotels themselves can arrange ground transportation and advise you on fares.

Tours. The state of Uttar Pradesh is working to cultivate tourism in Kanpur, and a tour guide can be helpful as a translator. In Lucknow, Tornos Destinations (India) (info@tornosindia.com or tel. 91 522 2346965) conducts day tours of Kanpur sites. Local guides with a comprehensive knowledge of 1857 Kanpur have been affiliated with the **Bicycling Society of Kanpur** which leads bicycle tours of the area and can be reached at 91 87545 79691 or via their Facebook page. Cars and motorcycles are discouraged within the cantonment.

Restaurants. The author prefers to eat street food while it is still sizzling, but **Kwality** at 16/19 Mall Road; **Dhuaan-Sheeska Kitchen** at 58 Tagore Road; and **Anaika's Food Joint** at 113/187 Khalasi Lane are usually safe bets.

Kanpur Sites

All Souls/Memorial Church. Located on Memorial Lane off Albert Lane in the centre of the Cantonment, the unmistakable enormous red-brick church, built to memorialize the Christian victims of the siege and massacres, stands on what was once the Entrenchment's north-west corner, over the redan. Its interior is lined with memorial plaques and its apse features marble panels listing all the local uprising's European and Eurasian fallen. On its grounds may be found numerous gravestones and memorials dating to the insurgency, and the still impressive remnant of the Memorial Well and Marochetti's angel that were moved here after Indian independence, have pride of place. The grounds can be visited during daylight hours without appointment, but to enter the church itself it is necessary to call the chaplain well ahead of time (at 91 84332 38429), or attend a 9 a.m. Sunday service. A donation to the church is recommended.

Wheeler's Entrenchment. Though perhaps half of the Entrenchment was marked off and preserved, there is little to orient a visitor to the original dimensions of the Entrenchment, except for the memorial stone to the first victims of the siege, which lies in what was once the south-western corner of the garden that lay behind the tile-roofed barrack. Looking westward you will see the well that provided water to the garrison and is the sole surviving Entrenchment structure.

Unfinished barracks and sepulchral well. The 'unfinished barracks' that Captain Moore and Lieutenant Thomson defended with the railwaymen were, in the end, finished and are still in use. Laid out on a bias 200 feet apart, they lie in a long row across and along Cambridge Road. Counting down from Hardinge Road, between the sixth and seventh barrackstands the memorial cross over the sepulchral well where the victims of the siege were deposited. To enter the memorial's enclosure, it is necessary to get permission from the Cantonment Board (tel. 91 51223 81285 or email at ceo@ cbkanpur.org.in.)

The route to Sati Chaura. Few 1857 sites are as unchanged and evocative as the route the garrison took to Sati Chaura Ghat, especially when traversed by foot. Known during the Raj as the 'Via Dolorosa of Empire', it begins, of course, at the Entrenchment and proceeds in something of a zigzag. Head north to the end of Memorial Lane, then turn right onto Hoolaganj Road, which, by its end, turns into Elgin Road. Turn right onto Cariappa Road, then left onto Nathusingh Road, then left onto Tagore Road, and after about 800 feet turn right onto Massacre Ghat Avenue and follow it and the adjacent ravine down to the river.

Hardeo Temple at Sati Chaura. The cross that used to identify Hardeo Temple (or the Boatmen's Temple) as the site of the attack is long gone, as is the hanging tree. But once you reach the river the temple is unmistakable. The pedestals from which the insurgents' leaders commanded the attack on the boats jut out towards the water. Since you are likeliest to visit in cool, dry weather, remember that at the time of the attack on 27 June, the Ganga had receded perhaps forty yards from the base of the temple steps and the river was shallow and riven with sandbars. The temple marks the centre of where the twenty-four boats were moored, with Wheeler's lead boat some 100 yards downriver, opposite what was once Colonel Williams's compound, from behind whose southernmost wall the sepoys emerged at a signal from their commanders. For those wanting to experience more of what the garrison endured, a boatman can be summoned to row you out into the river for a fee. (Note: There is a small Hindu religious establishment at Hardeo Temple, and you may be approached by one of its functionaries who largely depend on visitors' donations. As of this writing, a contribution of two dollars' worth of rupees should suffice.)

The Reading Room. The cantonment Reading Room or Library survived the uprising and was incorporated into the present-day Cawnpore Club at 87, Cantonment Road.

Assembly Rooms. The old Assembly Rooms, which at various times served as a storehouse for both the insurgency and the British, survived the uprising and now houses the main branch of the State

Bank of India at 16/101, The Mall. It is worth entering to get some idea of its dimensions and the prosperity of the European community that built it.

Lodge Harmony. Before the uprising, during Nana Sahib's ingratiation period, the local Masonic Lodge Harmony made him a member and, reputedly, the first Indian Mason. Convinced that the lodge was a 'house of magic' imbued with supernatural powers, he did not permit his soldiers to destroy it, nor did the British when they were clearing the way to meet Tatya Tope's attack. It survives on the Mall road opposite Nana Rao Park.

Savada House (or Savada Kothi) and the parade ground. Nana's headquarters at Savada House was demolished. Apparently, it stood in the southern crook of the modern-day junction of Hardinge Road and the Lakshmi Sehgal Flyover. A portion of the old racecourse—and the parade ground where the first Fatehgarh party and the prisoners from Wheeler's boat, among others, were executed—is now part of Kanpur Civil Airport.

Nana Rao Park and the Bibighar. There is some controversy over where, exactly, in Nana Rao Park the Bibighar well is situated. Thirty years ago, the author was told that the vast sandstone circle near the apex of the diamond-shaped park was where the Memorial Well once stood, but after his book was published and his documentary aired, he was notified by the British Association for Cemeteries in South Asia (BACSA) that the actual location was some yards north-west. I believe I was correct, but others, including Rosie Llewellyn-Jones, disagree. To find the site of the Memorial Well, look at the satellite image of Nana Rao Park on Google Maps and look at the area marked 'Company Bagh', a few paces north-north west of Tatya Tope's memorial.

The Bridge of Boats and Windham's entrenchment. Three bridges connect Kanpur to Awadh. The northernmost 'Old Ganga Bridge', an extension of Raebareli Road, is situated closest to where the Bridge of Boats spanned the Ganga, and takes the traveller to Unao, to which Havelock was driven back during his first attempts to relieve Lucknow. Imagine trying to transport thousands of rescued civilians and soldiers with their artillery and equipage across the Ganga on a floating, one-lane bridge in the monsoon, and you will get some idea of the obstacles with which Havelock, Outram and Campbell had to contend. If Windham House in OEF Colony in the cantonment is the site of Windham's entrenchment, it may be that the Bridge of Boats began further upstream than the Old Ganga Bridge. There is reportedly a museum at Windham House but the author has never been able to gain entry.

Bithur

Upstream from Kanpur, little remains of 1857 Bithur, and nothing of Nana Sahib's establishment. Much of the town has been rebuilt, but it retains its character as a place of pilgrimage. The Battle of Bithur is said to have been fought in an area between Hanuman Temple and the 'unfordable stream' that appears on the map of the battle.

Fatehgarh Site

Fatehgarh Fort is still standing, but off limits to visitors. The nawab's palace is now said to be part of the military hospital. The only site of remote interest is the Hospital Ghat from which the first band of fugitives departed.

The Battles

It would take a truly dauntless aficionado to try to retrace the route Havelock's column followed between Allahabad and Kanpur, and find the locations of the battles he fought with the insurgents at Fatehpur (Futtehpur on some maps), Aong, Pandu Nadi and Aherwa. Finding them requires determining what the southernmost edge of each of these towns and villages would have been in 1857, for the insurgents tended to meet Havelock in front of every town in which they took up positions. Taking these battles in chronological order, what appears as Futtehpur on nineteenth-century maps is now Fatehpur and lies about halfway between Allahabad and Kanpur; Aong is now Aung and lies about halfway between Fatehpur and Kanpur; the Battle of Pandu Nadi occurred where the Pandu river crosses the Grand Trunk Road; and Aherwa is now a neighbourhood of Kanpur's megalopolis and is called Ahirwan.

Notes

1. Taylor, P.G.O., *Remarks Delivered before a Gathering of Kanpur Historians,* January 1993; Waller, *Beyond the Khyber Pass,* pp. 137, 148.
2. Gough, Sir Hugh. *Old Memories*, p. 6; Lang, John. *Wanderings in India and other Sketches*, pp. 110-119; Lindsay, (Major) William. *Letters* ('Tomorrow, I am going to drive out with Sir J. Cheape to a pic-nic sort of party given by a native—gentleman—the adopted son of the peshwa—there is to be archery for the ladies in the afternoon—then a dinner party and finish with a Ball… I expect it to be a failure and a very stupid day.'); Misra, A.S. *Nana Sahib Peshwa,* p. 557.
3. Kaye, *A History of the Great Revolt,* 3:292; *The Presbyterian Banner,* 6 July 1911*;* Monckton Papers (Cambridge Center for South Asian Studies); Newton, *Historical Sketches;* Warren, *A Glance Backward,* pp. 13-14, 246; *Butler, Land of the Veda,* pp. 424, 427; Cosens and Wallace, *Fatehghar Camp*, especially pages pp. 1, 10-15, 17, 167; 178-181; 200; Gavin Jones, *Journal.*
4. MacKay, Aberigh, *Twenty-One Days in India*, pp. 119-125; Shepherd, William Jonah. *Guilty Men of 1857.* Halliday, *Emma, Letters*; Broadbridge, Lucy, Undated letter to the author. ('Many ex-India Anglo Indians of my generation and older have a very heightened sensitivity regarding their mixed-race origins because of the discrimination and prejudice they suffered at the hands of "pure" Europeans, and even snobbish Indians.')

5. Shepherd, William Jonah. *Narrative,* pp. 79, 94-5, 97-100, 116, 119, 136-137*;* Mary Ann (Ayah), in *Times of London,* 16 October 1857, p. 8; Depositions of Nana Ubbhunker, John Fitchett, Kalka Pershad, Peero, Futteh Singh, DeCruze, Cheda, Gobind Singh, Sheikh Elahee Buksh, Ghouse Mohammed, Cherunjoo Kuloo, Jankee Pershad in Forrest, *Selections from the Letters and Despatches and other State Papers in the Military Department of the Government of India: 1857-1858,* Vol. III.
6. Kaye. *A History of the Great Revolt,* 3:341-43, 348; Shepherd, *Narative,* p. 138; Neill quoted in Collier, *The Sound of Fury,* p. 210; Bingham in Hibbert, *The Great Mutiny,* p. 210; Neill, *Letter,* in Valbezen, *The English in India*, p. 166.
7. Tressider, John. *Mutiny Album*; Depositions as cited above in Forrest, *Selections from the Letters and Despatches and other State Papers in the Military Department of the Government of India: 1857-1858,* Vol. III.

Recommended Reading

SURPRISINGLY, THE MAGISTERIAL THREE-VOLUME *HISTORY of the Great Revolt* by J.W. Kaye and G.B. Malleson, published in the 1920s, lays much of the blame for the uprising at the Company's feet. Of the many general histories of the uprising, I recommend *The Great Mutiny* by Christopher Hibbert, and *The Last Mughal* by William Dalrymple. But the following are available books that directly relate to the uprising in Kanpur.

Our Bones Are Scattered by Andrew Ward.

The author's account of the Kanpur uprising, deemed by reviewers as definitive and drawing on hundreds of sources, including many never before tapped.

Currently out of print, but used paperback and hardcover copies of both the English (John Murray) and American (Henry Holt) 1996 editions are available via Alibris and Amazon.

Boxwallahs: The British in Cawnpore, 1857–1901 by Zoë Yalland. In this sequel to her *Traders and Nabobs,* the late author, who was born and raised in Kanpur, provides a detailed account of the uprising and its aftermath, with unique portraits of its merchants and industrialists.

Currently out of print, but hardcover copies of the 1994 London edition are available via Alibris and Amazon.

A Personal Narrative of the Outbreak and Massacre at Cawnpore During the Sepoy Revolt of 1857 by W.J. Shepherd.

William Jonah Shepherd, a fastidious Eurasian clerk in the Kanpur commissariat, was imprisoned by the insurgents after stealing out of the Entrenchment to spy. He lost his entire family in the uprising, and spent much of the rest of his life collecting information and answering inquiries from victims' families about their loved ones' fates. Though it is marred by his evangelistic condemnation of Indian religions, this is the best of the first-hand accounts of the uprising, providing vivid eyewitness testimony from behind both lines.

Paperback reprint of the 1879 edition by Andesite Press (London, 2015); also streamed for free online at Internet Archive.

The Story of Cawnpore by Mowbray Thomson.

The author was one of only two officers who survived the attack at Sati Chaura. He provides a sturdy narrative with an emphasis on the outer pickets in the unfinished barracks where he served during the siege. In an interview in 1858 he accused Wheeler of shirking his duty and taking no part in the defence, but pulled in his horns for this narrative. He does, however, make the same charge against a cowardly 'senior' officer who, a process of elimination establishes, was Deputy Judge-Advocate Edwin Wiggins.

Reprint of the 1859 edition by CreateSpace Independent Publishing Platform (London, 2015).

Cawnpore by G.O. Trevelyan.

Trevelyan wrote in 1894, when the British Empire was at its zenith and several survivors of the rebellion were still living. It is an elegantly written but unabashedly imperialist retelling based on his interpretations of various depositions, government records, the diary of Nanak Chand and Thomson's account. His interpretations are often fundamentally racist. For instance, he suspects Margaret Wheeler may have escaped because her mother, as he incorrectly claims, was a full-blooded Indian, pointing to it as the deciding factor for Margaret's different fate.

Paperback reprint of the 1894 edition by Alpha Editions (New Delhi, 2018).

Index

Acknowledgements

I WOULD LIKE TO THANK the United Service Institution (USI) of India—Centre for Military History and Conflict Studies (formerly Centre for Armed Forces Historical Research) for initiating the Battlefield Guide series.

I would also like to acknowledge the USI General Palit Military Studies Trust (GPMST) for their assistance in acquiring an illustration for inclusion in the guide.

In addition to the many people who assisted me in writing my book, *Our Bones Are Scattered*, the author is indebted to Rosie Llewellyn-Jones, the author of the Lucknow volume in this series, and to Mark Probett, a descendant of William Morris Probett and family who were killed at Kanpur in 1857, for donating images from his extensive collection for this volume.

Other Books in the Series

The city of Lucknow was the epicentre of the uprising of 1857.

In *Lucknow, 1857*—part of a new series of books on India's historic battles—historian Rosie Llewellyn-Jones examines the conflict in detail, from the British annexation of Awadh to the Indian response and the subsequent revolt by sepoys. The defeat of a unit of the East India Company's army at Chinhat led immediately to the siege of the extensive British Residency in the heart of the city. Here, nearly 3,000 people—British, Indian and Anglo-Indian—held out for four and a half months. The winter saw huge defensive barricades being built around Lucknow, but with their superior firepower, the British recapture was the inevitable outcome.

This richly illustrated field guide draws on Llewellyn-Jones's intimate knowledge of the city to paint a vivid picture of the events that unfolded in this historic urban battlefield.

About the United Service Institution of India

ESTABLISHED IN 1870 BY MAJOR General Sir Charles MacGregor in Shimla (then Simla), the United Service Institution of India (USI) is a national security and defence services think tank based in New Delhi. Its aim is the 'furtherance of interest and knowledge in the art, science and literature of the defence services'. It is located at Vasant Vihar, New Delhi, from where it has been operating since 1996.

About the Centre for Military History and Conflict Studies (Formerly Centre for Armed Forces Historical Research)

THE CENTRE WAS ESTABLISHED IN December 2000 under the aegis of the USI for encouraging the objective study of all facets of Indian military history with a special emphasis on the history of the Indian Armed Forces. It focuses on diverse aspects of the history of Indian military evolution, policies and practices—strategic, tactical, logistical, organisational and socio-economic, as well as the field of contemporary conflict studies.

About the Author

Andrew Ward was raised in India and has returned to it as a photographer, novelist, and award-winning historian. His novel *The Blood Seed* takes place in Kanpur, and his history of the Kanpur uprising, *Our Bones Are Scattered*, was universally praised by reviewers in India, Britain, and the United States. He lives in California.